WORLD WAR II
RADIO HEROES

Letters of Compassion

LISA L. SPAHR
WITH AUSTIN CAMACHO

Reviews of World War II
Radio Heroes: Letters of Compassion

"Movies, documentaries, and books by the thousands have been created over the 60-plus years since the end of WWII. Yet Lisa Spahr has discovered a compelling part of the war that has received little attention. *World War II Radio Heroes* tells the story of how thousands of Americans stayed awake by short-wave radios throughout the night, wrote down the names of captured POWs broadcast by the Germans, and wrote postcards, letters and telegrams to the prisoners' worried families.

Broadcasts from or about a POW touched all who listened because that could be their husband, son or brother in the hands of the enemy. The primary purpose of these enemy radio broadcasts was to undermine the morale of the American people. Propaganda was a weapon, and the best way to avoid any risk of it having an effect was to turn off the radio.

The listeners that Lisa Spahr writes about ignored the propaganda embedded in the broadcasts, and they captured the golden nuggets—the bits of information and recordings of their fellow citizens who were POWs.

Lisa Spahr's book captures Americans at their best. *World War II Radio Heroes* brings to life this almost forgotten story about World War II, and shows Americans for what they are: an energetic, compassionate and free people."

MATTHEW PUGLISI
GULF WAR VETERAN, U.S. MARINE CORPS RESERVES, RETIRED

"Lisa Spahr's *Radio Heroes* bears witness to the kindness and patriotism of a mostly forgotten band of short-wave listeners and amateur radio operators who monitored Nazi Germany's radio broadcasts for news of captured U.S. service personnel, passing on information and hope to the families of the missing. It is a very personal story of discovery, beginning with her grandfather's 'war trunk' and growing into a search for the few remaining radio heroes who had written so many letters of compassion."

JAMES D. WALRATH, PH.D.
K3BEN

"The kindness of strangers is evident in the efforts of each individual engaged in POW Monitoring, their dedication provided comfort to so many at a very difficult time. This book serves as fitting tribute to individuals who made a difference in the lives of so many. They brought hope, relief and above all compassion to the families of service men and women fighting for our freedom. Clearly, the loyal listeners and relayers made a difference in the lives of so many and they are truly heroes. These heroes are aptly honored within this book for their letters of compassion."

FRAN HACKETT
MEMBER, ADVISORY COMMITTEE ON
OIF/OEF VETERANS AND THEIR FAMILIES

"Lisa Spahr's book *WWII Radio Heroes: Letters of Compassion* struck a chord with me, because one of my most prized possessions is a 1943 letter written by a 21-year old Marine corporal from a Pacific island to his newborn girl—me!

Wartime letters are very special, and those Lisa writes about—the caring attempts of strangers to notify mothers, fathers, wives, and sweethearts that their loved ones *were* alive and prisoners of war—are among the most special I've read.

I was particularly interested in the Short-Wave Amateur Monitors Club, organized by Mrs. Don Yant in 1943. Its purpose was to ensure that someone would be monitoring German broadcasts [entitled *Calling Back Home*] over Berlin Radio every single night of the week in order to gather the names of the captured so that no POW family would wait in agony, wondering if their loved one was alive or dead.

I recommend *WWII Radio Heroes* highly to anyone who has served, as well as anyone who has waited in anxiety while a loved one served in harm's way on a hostile shore."

REV. MITZI MANNING
COLONEL, U.S. MARINE CORPS, RETIRED

"I expect that many people have never heard the heartwarming story of the men and women across America who regularly monitored Nazi short-wave broadcasts to learn the fate of American GIs taken prisoner by the Germans. After sorting the information out from the crackle of atmospherics and man-made interference, these great folks would pass the information on to the loved ones back home. What a great story!

As a life-long amateur radio operator (Ham), veteran, and child of the '40s, I'm glad to learn this fascinating story and specifically the folks who made sure that 'no POW family would go without notice.' Lisa Spahr has added a valuable dimension to the story of the many ways in which Americans contributed to the World War II effort."

HONORABLE CHARLES L. CRAGIN
FORMER CHAIRMAN, BOARD OF VETERANS' APPEALS
AND SENIOR DEFENSE OFFICIAL

For all of the unsung heroes of the greatest generation—
may you receive your due recognition and our gratitude forever

and

For my family—
I am lucky to have you. I love you.

The author has attempted to identify and locate the copyright owners of the letters
and related material included in this edition of *World War II Radio Heroes Letters
of Compassion*. Grateful acknowledgement is made to individuals who have kindly
granted permission for the use of their materials in this edition of *World War II
Radio Heroes Letters of Compassion*. If there are instances where proper credit is not
given, the author will gladly make necessary corrections in subsequent printings.

ISBN 978-0-9762181-7-3

Printed in the United States
Graphic design by Dave Williams

Contents

Acknowledgments

This book would not have been possible had it not been for the men, women and children who tuned in their short-wave radios in 1943, listening for news of our frontline heroes—and then spending their time, money and energy forwarding every last word they could to the families so desperate for news. Specifically, Flavius Jankauskas, Morton Bardfield, Ruby Yant, Irene Walters and Sanford Lowe—I am humbled and my life has been forever enriched to have learned about the amazing deeds of you and your fellow radio listeners. My gratitude will be yours forever.

I am also grateful to my family—Mom, Ida and Charlie—for keeping the trunk and its contents so that I could explore it when I was ready. Too often these treasures lose their places in attics and basements and end up at yard sales. I will never look at such items: military portraits, letters from war, or selective service cards, the same way after this incredible journey. Thank you also for being such a supportive force in my life. You've always encouraged me to dream big and live life to the fullest. That encouragement allowed me to approach this project with zest and vigor and without one ounce of doubt that it could be done. I'll always love you for this and so much more.

John Sommer, how lucky I am to know you and have worked for you. You are a model of a true American. Your dedication to our men and women who have served is unsurpassed. Your enthusiasm for this project, and all of the tasks you completed without much fanfare, will always be close to my heart. You helped me make this happen!

I will be grateful always to my team, Team Camacho. Austin and Denise have guided me through this process, offered their expert advice and personal opinions, and supported me wholeheartedly in this journey to produce my first non-technical publication. I'm sure I was a handful at several junctures, but they kept their cool and urged me to make better decisions and set more realistic deadlines! Their assistance was always helpful and spot on—they know this process well. And, they never asked anything of me. I never would have guessed, having met Austin many years earlier as we criss-crossed the country visiting military bases together, that he and his wife would become my family away from home. But they did. I couldn't be more glad. Thank you both—for everything.

Each time I approached another person, usually to ask for their help, and discuss the project, they welcomed me. This book was written and completed with a few pennies and a lot of volunteers. I am thankful to all the contributors and people behind the scenes, specifically: Morton Bardfield for his weekly packages of relevant information; Dave Williams for his excitement about this project and his excellent design skills; Craig Fischer for his editing genius (where were you when I struggled through English comp?); Lloyd Rich for his legal eye and taxi service and Donn Nemchick for his "on the ground" marketing plan. There are dozens of others I hope to thank personally.

Finally, my gratitude is owed to the many people I reached in my search for authors of the 1943 postcards and letters. Although too many years have gone by and I didn't have great luck at finding them, I was continually met with kindness and enthusiasm by those who happened to receive my letters and calls. People thanked me for my project, saying I was inspiring them. Others reminisced about the author of the letters, and told me about their lives. All were helpful, warm, gracious, and full of humility. Thank You.

Lisa L. Spahr
Author

FOREWORD

The many battles, large and small, that took place during World War II, and the tales of heroic deeds by those who fought those battles, have been chronicled in an untold number of books and movies that to this date continue to be written and produced. The history of that era is also replete with stories of "the war at home" and how this great nation pulled together to support the troops who were fighting overseas, and to conserve precious resources needed to equip and sustain our armed forces. Those of us born during or just after the war have heard stories from family and friends of the Victory Gardens, war bonds, scrap metal and rubber drives, and the rationing of food, gasoline, nylon stockings, and other products. We know of the Gold Star Banners and the Blue Star Banners that hung in the windows of families who had lost loved ones in the war, or who had kin serving in the military.

I'm something of a student of WWII. I was raised by and among veterans who were part of what Tom Brokaw so appropriately designated "the Greatest Generation." And I spent most of my childhood and all of my adult years in, around and part of The American Legion. So I considered my basic knowledge of WWII to be fairly complete—until I met Lisa Spahr for lunch one day in March of 2007. Lisa spoke poignantly of her grandfather, of the experiences she shared with him during her childhood, and of her sadness at his passing when she was eleven years of age. Lisa told me that her grandfather had served in the Army during World War II and was captured by the Germans in 1943, and that he spent the remainder of the war as a POW. She then fast-forwarded to 2006, when she began to examine the contents of her grandfather's "war trunk," which contained relics of his WWII service and, especially, his prisoner of war experience.

Lisa's enthusiasm heightened as she told me about her discovery of "the letters"—a collection of letters and postcards, addressed to her grandfather's mother by complete strangers, informing her of her son's capture by the Germans. The letter-writers had heard about Lisa's grandfather's POW status on the radio—through propaganda radio broadcasts that the Germans transmitted to the world on short-wave frequencies. Apparently the Germans thought it would demoralize the Allies to hear about their sons and brothers and husbands who had been captured. In fact, however, many American families were *relieved* to hear that their soldier had been captured, because otherwise they had to face the possibility that their loved one was missing in action.

It became apparent to me that I *didn't* know about some of the efforts of those who fought the war at home. Lisa told me about the magnitude of the phenomenon known as message relay or POW monitoring, and I was astounded to learn that thousands of concerned Americans sent hundreds of thousands of messages to the families of POWs to make sure they knew the status of their loved ones. Lisa's great-grandmother alone received 69 letters and postcards. Some who wrote to the Spahr family mentioned they were sending hundreds of other such letters. What an incredible effort to reach out to families of those servicemen captured by the enemy!

During her extensive research in preparing the manuscript for this book, Lisa uncovered a treasure trove of information about wartime compassion that, until this time, had been largely unknown. She is to be commended for bringing this story to light and sharing it with us.

John F. Sommer, Jr.
Executive Director
The American Legion

CHAPTER 1

Discovery of the Trunk

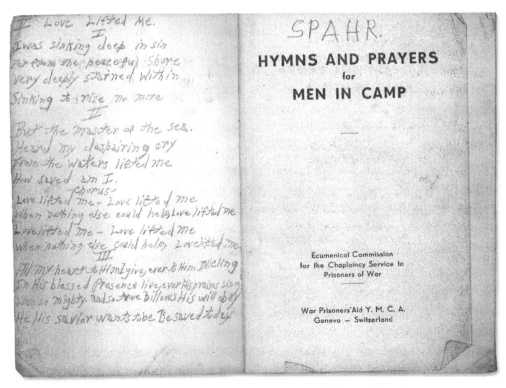

My grandfather's POW Hymn and Prayer Book

always thought there was little to be discovered about my family. I was an only child raised in a small town in southern Pennsylvania. My mother had only one sister and one brother, neither of whom ever married. Therefore, I am the only one in my generation in our immediate family. My grandmother passed on when I was five years of age, and my grandfather died when I was 11.

Because I never met my father, my grandfather and uncle filled the masculine roles in my young life. I knew that my grandfather served in the U.S. Army during World War II and that he served most of his time as a prisoner of war. My favorite memories of him are the frequent fishing trips we took on the lake at Pinchot Park.... riding around in his bright red Volkswagen Beetle talking on the CB radio (my "handle" was Wonder Woman, of course).... and one short-lived attempt at rabbit hunting (when I discovered the woods didn't have a suitable bathroom for a little girl, I asked my grandfather to take me home right away, which—kindly—he did). One memory that I could have done without was witnessing his slow decline in health. Heroes aren't supposed to die—and certainly not from cancer.

So growing up, I always thought of my family as a small one, and I knew my few relatives well, so how could there be any surprises in store for me? But recently, I found I was wrong; there was still room for discovery.

I always knew that my aunt and uncle had a "war trunk" that contained items my grandfather brought back with him from Germany. Perhaps it was out of respect for him, or for his privacy, but I never rushed to the trunk to explore its contents. Maybe I didn't want to think of him during wartime, a prisoner so far from home. Perhaps I worried that I would discover something about him that would alter my impression of who he was—after all, war is something I couldn't fathom. I could only imagine the atrocities that men had gone through. And staying away from the trunk was in line with the way my family often behaved. We aren't necessarily ones to ask personal questions of each other or tread in each other's personal affairs. So the trunk remained a treasure that would go unexplored by me until one day in 2006—six decades after World War II ended.

I suppose it was a measure of time coupled with the desire to learn as much as possible about my ever-so small family that drew me to investigating that trunk. Although our deceased loved ones are no longer among us, it dawned on me that there was still so much to embrace—and learn. Further, the need to be close to my grandfather may have been what finally called me to look in the trunk. After all, "Pappy" was the greatest man to grace the earth, in my eyes at least, and I missed him. I often wonder how he would feel about the woman I have grown to become. How would he have felt when I made mistakes—some small, some not so small? In any case, on two occasions, months apart from each other, I asked my aunt and uncle's permission to go into the trunk. They were both overjoyed that I was interested, but at the same time filled with sadness that whatever difficulties my grandfather experienced in the War would again be opened up and explored. After all, they missed him too. We all did. My aunt and uncle feel my grandfather's absence often—they still live in the house where he and my grandmother raised them. Not a day goes by that they don't think of him, imagining him tinkering around the house like it was yesterday.

My grandfather's German Phrase Book

The first time I opened the trunk I was in awe to find Pappy's uniform. I was quickly reminded that he was such a slender man. He was also handsome, and to this day, I am filled with great pride each time I see pictures of him. To touch his uniform felt like such a special treat. The trunk contained a hymnal and prayer book for men in camp, a restricted German phrase book,

Pappy's immunization record, various war documents, POW bulletins from the Red Cross—and *"the letters."*

Ah, the letters. I couldn't make much of them at first, but it appeared that a large number of people, none of whom I could identify, had written letters to my great-grandmother letting her know that my grandfather had been captured and was being held as a POW. How did they know this? Well, it seems that the German government was broadcasting propaganda all over the world in an effort to demoralize the Allied forces, and part of this propaganda

Prisoners of War Bulletin, published by the American Red Cross for families of POWs

campaign involved interviewing American soldiers who had been captured. The soldiers were allowed to state their names and hometowns on the radio, and sometimes to give a short message to their families. And what happened was this: Scores of Americans, listening to the German propaganda on short-wave radio, heard my grandfather's name and hometown, and took it upon themselves to write to my great-grandmother to let her know that her son apparently was not missing in action, because they had heard him on the radio. All of these dear people wanted to give my great-grandmother a measure of comfort and perhaps ease her worrying about her son a bit.

I didn't focus on these letters the first time I looked in the trunk. Perhaps the overwhelming nature of seeing all of the treasures that belonged to my beloved grandfather was too much at first. It wasn't until months later, on a subsequent visit home, that I again asked to revisit the trunk.

This time, I asked my aunt and uncle if I could take home a few items so that I could explore them in private. I took as many as I could, and over the coming months, I started to get the feeling that I was on to something very powerful—a discovery of a magnitude I hadn't known before. From Easter through December of 2006 I held the letters, read each one, and chronicled and preserved them as best I could. They were so beautiful, each of them, with a very formal writing style, clear penmanship and perfect grammar. The authors clearly attempted to get each word about my grandfather, spoken from thousands of miles away, exactly as it was said. Although written by a stranger, each letter had a personal feel to it, so poignant, so sad and yet uplifting. After reading and rereading each letter, I began my journey to find some of those kind souls who wrote them in 1943.

To the extent that I could find any of the people who wrote these letters, or their family members, I wanted to let them know how much their kindness must have meant to my great-grandmother, who was a widow during World War II, with five of her sons at war. I could only imagine what must have gone through her head as she received her first, second, third, twentieth, sixtieth, and finally sixty-ninth letter. All were from strangers who found it in their hearts to write to her. They wrote during a time when everyone, it appeared, was short on money—yet full of hope that the war would come to an end so that peace could be restored to all who were affected. These wonderful people took it upon themselves to reach out to my great-grandmother then, and I was determined to try to reach out to them now—to say thank you. Thank you for your priceless gift to my family back in 1943. How else could I acknowledge such kindness?

CHAPTER 2

A Reflection on Times Past

My grandfather, Robert May Spahr, and his sister, Martha (Marty) Spahr

Robert May Spahr was born August 16, 1916, the sixth of 12 children, to Jacob and Martha Spahr. Robert was the sixth-generation Spahr born in America; his ancestor, Hanns Michael Spaar, had left Germany in 1742 on the ship *Robert Alice* bound for Philadelphia.

Robert's father, Jacob, was a very progressive man of his time. Family history has it that he chose a vocation for each of his 12 children early on in their development, rather than assume they'd naturally follow in his footsteps. He wanted each of his children to have every opportunity possible to succeed in life.

Jacob and Martha bought a farm in the New Mexico Territory, but later traded it for a Kissel touring car and returned to York County, Pa. to purchase Jacob's father's farm. But Jacob died young, at the age of 59, eight months before his youngest son was born. My Great Aunt Martha ("Marty"), her mother's namesake and a younger sibling to my grandfather, once impressed upon me how difficult this was for my great-grandmother—she was a widow with 11 children and a 12th on the way, about to face the Great Depression.

After losing her husband, Martha had to make the difficult decision to split the family up to ensure that all the children could adequately be cared for.

My grandfather and several of his siblings were sent off to local farms to work for room and board. Great Aunt Marty tells a story about a farmer who wanted to whip my grandfather for something he had done wrong. Marty stepped up and said, "If you want to whip Robert, you'll have to whip each one of us." The farmer didn't want that kind of trouble out of his help, so he sent them back to their mother to find another place to live. Great Aunt Marty often told me that story in the last years of her life, still laughing aloud each time she told it. She spoke so fondly of Robert. She said he was always the one to care for the children after school. He cooked, cleaned, worked long hours and never asked for anything in return or complained.

Of the eight males in my grandfather's generation of Spahrs, five served in World War II. Robert signed up for selective service on October 16, 1941 and joined the war effort on May 28, 1942 at the age of 25. He joined the U.S. Army, Headquarters Company,

1st Battalion, 26th Infantry Regiment. He spent 29 months in the European theater of operations. He was captured in Tunisia, North Africa and served 26 of his 29 months as a POW in Germany (ironically, where our ancestors came from generations before).

My grandfather's Selective Service Card

The word of Robert's capture was relayed to my great-grandmother, Martha, in two ways: a telegram from the War Department received May 8, 1943 at 6:09 a.m., and 69 postcards and letters from radio listeners all across the country, the first of which was postmarked on May 8, 1943 at 5:30 p.m.—*the same day as the official telegram!* She received many more of these notices in the coming days and weeks following the War Department telegram.

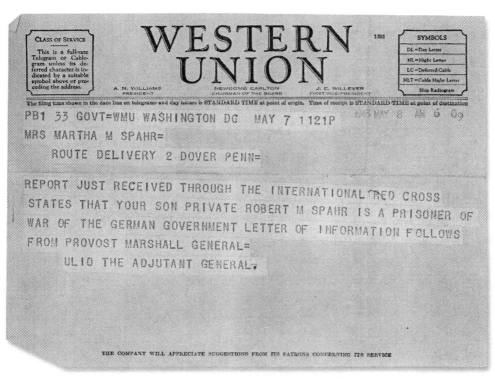

Telegram from the War Department in 1943 regarding my grandfather's capture and imprisonment

During his imprisonment, Robert kept a log of letters he received and those he wrote. When I found this log in the trunk, I realized how important it must have been to him to receive mail from home. He must have been quite homesick, to keep such a meticulous log of his correspondence from family members a world away. There were

From	No.	wrote			Received		
mother.	23	Oct.	25.	1943	Feb.	21,	1944
Roman Spahr.	24	Oct.	26.	1943.	Feb.	21.	1944
Roman Spahr.	25	Nov.	10.	1943.	Mar.	3.	1944
Jacob and Brownie.	26	Nov.	3.	1943.	Mar.	3.	1944
Kathryne Myers.	27	Nov.	16.	1943.	Mar	14.	1944
Kathryn Myers.	28	Nov.	26.	1943.	Mar.	13.	1944
Richard Myers.	29	Nov.	30.	1943.	Mar.	13.	1944
mother.	30	Dec.	10.	1943.	April	6.	1944.
Kathryn Myers.	31	Dec.	17.	1943	April	6.	1944
Kathryn Myers.	32	Jan.	15.	1944	April.	6.	1944
Kathryn Myers.	33	Nov.	23.	1943	April	6.	1944.
Kathryn Myers.	34	Dec.	29.	1943.	April.	15.	1944
Ralph. Crone.	35	Jan.	15	1944.	April.	15.	1944.
Gredon Diller.	36	Feb.	10.	1944	June	2.	1944.
Roman Spahr.	37	Mar.	13,	1944.	June.	13.	1944.
Roman Spahr.	38	Dec.	1.	1943,	June.	22.	1944
Kathryn Myers.	39	Jan.	30.	1944.	June.	22.	1944.
Kathryn Myers.	40	Jan	23.	1944.	July	2.	1944
Roman Spahr.	41	Jan	6.	1944.	July	2.	1944
Kathryn Myers.	42	Feb.		1944.	July	14.	1944
Kathryn Myers.	43	Mar.	1.	1944.	July	14.	194
Roman Spahr.	44	Mar.	12.	1944.	July	14.	194

My grandfather's log: letters incoming
and outgoing from prison camp

many reports of mail going undelivered to POWs for a multitude of reasons. I am very thankful that my grandfather's mail appeared to have been sent and received with little interruption. I can only guess that a single letter was likely to sustain a solder, particularly an imprisoned one, for a long time.

From.	78	wrote.			Received.		
Roman Spa	45	april.	6,	1944,	July	18.	1944,
Roman Spah	46	april.	11.	1944,	July	18.	1944.
Ralph Crane.	47	april.	12.	1944.	July	18.	1944.
Roman Spah	48	april.	17.	1944.	July	18.	1944.
Kathryn my	49	mar.	24.	1944	July	27.	1944
Roman Spa	50	april	11.	1944	July	27.	1944
Roman Spa	51	april	16.	1944	aug	9.	1944
Roman Spa	52	april	3.	1944	aug	28.	1944
Kathryn my	53	april	3.	1944	aug	28.	1944
Kathryn my	54	april	11.	1944	aug	28.	1944
Kathryn my	55	april	24.	1944	aug	28.	1944
Kathryn my	56	april	20.	1944	oct.	6.	1944
Kathryn my	57	april.	15.	1944	oct	6	1944
Roman Spa	58	may	15.	1944	nov.	1.	1944
Kathryn my	59	may	16.	1944	nov.	1.	1944
Kathryn m	60	may	13.	1944	nov.	3.	1944
Kathryn m	61	June	21.	1944	nov.	3.	1944
Kathryn my	62	June	27.	1944	nov.	3	1944
Kathryn m	63	July	10.	1944	nov.	3.	1944
Kathryn m	64	July.	19.	1944	nov.	3,	1944
Kathryn m	65	may	4.	1944	nov.	26.	1944
mrs. Effie. mu	66	July	19.	1944	nov.	26,	1944

Mail was such a treasure, but at the same time it often appeared very sterile as a result of censors reading it and omitting information they didn't want the prisoners to receive. Letter-writers learned to avoid saying anything that might catch the eye of the censors. Here is one of the first letters sent by my grandmother, Kathryn, to her boyfriend at the time, my grandfather.

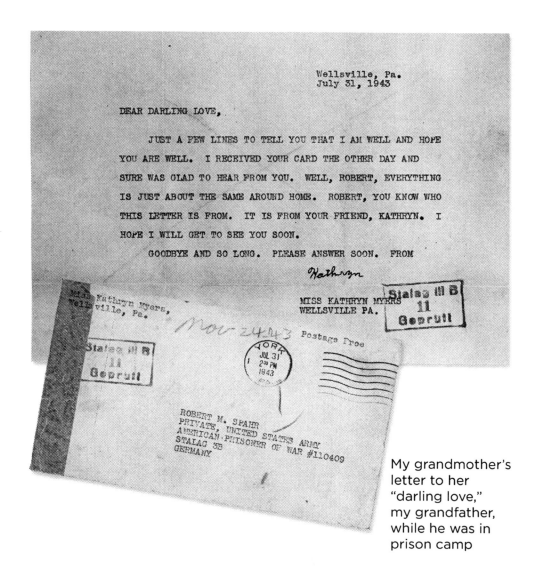

My grandmother's letter to her "darling love," my grandfather, while he was in prison camp

CHAPTER 3

A GRANDDAUGHTER'S QUEST

My grandfather and I in 1975

F or months I held and read the nearly 70 letters from strangers all over the United States written during May 1943. I came to understand that there was a phenomenon known as *message relay* or *POW monitoring,* in which individuals and organizations took it upon themselves to alert POW families of their loved ones' capture and transport to prison camps. Many of these men and women were doing this for hundreds, sometimes thousands of families.

Learning more about this process was like unwrapping a set of Russian dolls. There was always more to explore, and my astonishment never dwindled. I had never heard of message relays before. I asked friends, and no one had ever heard of this process. The fact that so few appeared to know about this led me to write this book. The story had to be told.

Researching this practice was quite challenging. There is little information available regarding message relays during World War II. I was able to locate a few short-wave amateur radio operators and related Websites that documented these letters and postcards to POW families. One such person was Lieutenant Colonel Morton Bardfield, who highlighted his experience as a young man in his teens who listened to the German radio program called *Calling Back Home*. He immersed himself in writing to families of POWs to alert them of their loves ones' status, and worked as a paperboy to earn money to buy and send the postcards. Lt. Col. Bardfield didn't write to my family, but he had wonderful stories about the people he did contact and their kindness to him over the years.

Calling Back Home

Calling Back Home was a nightly radio program that was broadcast from Berlin, Germany on Radio Berlin, a station playing propaganda day and night. POWs' names, next of kin, and a short message would be read over the airwaves.

Some of the postcards and letters to my great-grandmother clearly note that a woman "who spoke perfect English" read this information. From my research I believe this woman was Axis Sally, also known as Midge on the Mike, real name Mildred Gillars, who was

"No Family Ever Complained About Receiving More than One Letter":
A Teenage Boy Uses His New Radio for a Compassionate Mission

Like most kids growing up in the 1940s, my family evening entertainment was just an AM radio console. Most nights I enjoyed programs like "The Lone Ranger" or "Jack Armstrong— The All-American Boy." For me, World War II was a distant struggle, and a world apart. But that changed on my 13th birthday when I received an all-band radio. The reality of the war entered my Dorchester, Mass., home when I began to pick up German announcers each evening on Berlin Radio, reading in clear English the names, messages and home addresses of American prisoners.

It would seem that no American could "discover" these important messages and just switch off the short-wave without sending a note to some parent that their son was alive, no longer missing in action. So it seemed natural to me to mail out these nightly POW reports to the parents on penny postcards. (I couldn't afford 3-cent stamps from my paper route earnings!) During the war, I wasn't aware that anyone else might also be notifying the parents or wives, so my postcards became just as important to me as playing soldier or doing my homework.

Knowing now that other radio listeners were also sending out notifications, I am sure that no family ever complained about receiving more than one joyous letter.

Lt. Col. Morton Bardfield, USAR, ret.
Brookline, Mass.

later tried for treason for her role during the war. Axis Sally would interview prisoners in camps, disguising herself as a Red Cross worker, to get information from prisoners, only to intermix the audio interviews with propaganda on the radio airwaves.[1] Other letters to my great-grandmother say that the soldiers themselves spoke over the radio. One writer said that she heard my grandfather give his information. I believe that either my grandfather was in fact interviewed by Axis Sally, or perhaps by a counterpart, Lord Haw-Haw, a British citizen who participated in propaganda on Radio Berlin and who read my grandfather's name and message. Whoever announced the information and for whatever reason, it appears likely that the radio programs were repeated, with POWs' names being read more than once in a given week.

The American Legion Magazine featured an article in October 1943[2] which warned radio listeners and those who received letters and postcards about these radio announcements to be wary of such communications, because American officials were aware that methods of propaganda were being used. The information at times was faulty and meant only to draw more listeners. The American Legion article laid out the official and unofficial processes whereby families could learn about their loved ones' status. The War Department received its information from the Red Cross, the Protecting Powers, the Vatican, and intercepted radio messages (which could be problematic as noted above). The article went on to give an indication of how many people were involved in this effort and how many names were being relayed through all of these various channels. Between 5,000 and 6,000 people, mostly volunteers, worked for the International Red Cross in Switzerland, handling nearly 60,000 pieces of mail daily. The Swiss office would get the information from the Nazi

---

1. Harper, Dale. (no date) Mildred Elizabeth Sisk: American-Born Axis Sally. www.historynet.com.
2. Rathbone, A.D. Johnny Doughboy, Prisoner. The American Legion Magazine. October 1943.

Intelligence Agency and then pass the information on to the Provost Marshal's Office in Washington, D.C. The Provost's Office would then, likely, send word to the families of the POWs.

I located an article published in a 1998 Disabled American Veterans' Magazine that featured another radio hero, Irene Walters, who listened to Radio Berlin nightly while her children were asleep and her husband was at work.[3] She happened to tune in to Axis Sally one night and began writing letters, not knowing that anyone else was doing the same. She "saw the opportunity to bring hope to worried families." She would often stay up until 3 or 4 a.m. to get all of the postcards written. She said that she didn't write down any ailments or wounds the boys were said to have suffered, only that they were alive—the information she felt she would want to know if she were a soldier's parent. She received more than 1,000 grateful messages in return! One father of a POW was so appreciative he donated hundreds of dollars in her name to the American Red Cross.

I was also able to locate some written work by an ex-POW, Captain George Duffy, who wrote about his discovery of the letters his mother received during his capture and imprisonment by the Japanese.[4] Captain Duffy noted that to the upset of the government, hundreds of "ex-officio intelligence agents" and thousands of anxious family members were listening to enemy radio programs to learn about loved ones and other prisoners. He went on to say he had heard that the Federal Bureau of Investigation had investigated these "ex-officio agents" and concerned citizen listeners on suspicion of being spies. (This phenomenon also was brought to my attention by the son of one of the people who wrote to my great-grandmother.) Coincidentally, one of the men who wrote to Captain Duffy's mother, Sanford Lowe, also wrote to my family. He is reported to

---

3. Wilborn, Thom. Short-wave radio monitors let families know of their capture. DAV Magazine, July/August 1998, p. 10.
4. Duffy, George. (no date) Honoring those who listened. www.usmm.org/duffyhonoring.html.

have sent more than 10,000 letters during the war. He was a member of the Short Wave Amateur Monitor's Club, which I describe later in this book.

Axis Sally's counterpart in the Pacific was known as Tokyo Rose, a name given to multiple women who could be heard on the radio in the Pacific Theater delivering propaganda. One of the women known as Tokyo Rose, Iva Toguri, was pardoned by President Ford in 1977. She had reportedly found herself stranded in Japan when the war broke out. She used parody as a way to sabotage her radio show and was providing the allies with food and medication.[5]

General Description of the Letters

Each letter was unique in its own way. They were written by men and women; young and old; some writers chose to remain anonymous, but most proudly offered their names. Some requested return letters, to ensure their letters were received. The length varied from a few lines to a few pages. They were both handwritten and typed. All of the letters had a variation of this one phrase within: "Have arrived safely in Germany as a prisoner. Robert."

As a psychologist, I am fascinated by the content of the letters. What was the greatest motivation for these people to listen to the radio so avidly and take such pains to contact family members? Was it a need to play a direct role in the war effort? Was it knowing the comfort their letters would bring to the families? These questions led me to consider another I had pondered quite often: What would my great-grandmother have thought and felt when the letters began to come in?

---

5. New York Times. December 10, 2001. War on the radio: Tokyo Rose, Axis Sally, and Hanoi Hannah broadcast propaganda aimed at turning the hearts of lonely U.S. Soldiers. By Sean Price.

Some writers made a special effort to comfort my great-grand-mother by saying things like, "He said 'Don't worry, that he loves you, and that he is being treated well.'" I wept thinking about my great-grandmother receiving and reading each letter. Was she over-whelmed? Overjoyed to know he was alive, or filled with dread that he was a prisoner? I suppose it was a bit of both. And what was my grandfather thinking, feeling, experiencing as a POW? When he returned home, did he and my great-grandmother discuss all of the letters she received?

Unfortunately, with the passing of my great-grandmother and grandfather, I'll never know the answers to these questions.

I was so moved by the kindness of all of these people that I made it my task to see if any of the original authors could be found, or at least their next of kin. With precious spare time in the evenings, I began my quest to find the letter-writers. It occurred to me that what I was doing was similar to the work of the letter-writers, who spent their evenings back in 1943 writing letters to strangers.

I turned to the Internet for a name search. I made lists of all the authors and cities of origin. From there I let Internet search engines do the work, running each name in the respective city. Of course, there were some names that simply were not found. In other cases, common names like "Johnson" resulted in thousands of "hits." I chose the names and cities that I thought offered the greatest chance of being matched. I wrote a letter explaining my mission and offering my sincere thanks in the event that my letter might reach any of its targets.

I sent the letter on the next page to approximately 75 people. Some letters were sent to multiple people with the same last name; I was hoping to get a match or lead on the author with the same last name. This effort took only a few weeks. I began receiving telephone calls, emails, and return-to-sender responses immediately. I would have been satisfied with just one positive response. I received nearly a dozen.

RE: WWII Letters

Dear _____

I was going through my grandfather's WWII trunk and discovered dozens of letters and postcards from strangers all across the country, alerting my great-grandmother of my grandfather's POW status. I had not heard of this process of listening via short-wave radio and alerting next of kin to soldiers' capture and imprisonment, until I found these letters and postcards.

I know that I'm unlikely to find the persons who were so generous to do this, but I wanted to try. I have addresses and names from 1943 which I am using to try to send a letter of thanks to them or their next of kin, if I can find them.

These postcards and letters have become a treasure to my family. All of us are moved to tears when we read and reread them. Strangers were reaching out to others in hopes of bringing some comfort—that their soldier was alive—to families living each day to hear such news. The letters must have been bittersweet to the recipients, because they then knew that their soldier was alive, but he was a prisoner. My grandfather was a prisoner for 26 months.

One such letter or postcard received was from _(name)_ located in the _(city/town of…)_. If this person is a family member of yours or you know about them, please express and accept my deepest gratitude for their efforts in 1943. Their kindness has been shared for generations within my family and will continue to be for many more to come.

We can only hope that people still possess this sort of kindness toward one another. This united effort to look out for one another has not been matched since WWII. Hopefully, that will one day change.

My sincerest regards to you and your family.

Lisa Spahr
Granddaughter of a WWII POW

One such piece of correspondence I received was from the Fike family. Mr. John Fike, Omaha, Neb., wrote to my great-grandmother on May 9, 1943 to alert her that my grandfather had been taken as a prisoner and was moving from one camp to another in Germany.

My letter to Mr. Fike's family in May 2006 reached his son, Charles. His letter is on the following page. I was especially interested in the FBI's visit to the Fike home, described in the second-to-last paragraph.

Dear Mrs. Spahar —
Saturday May 8th from 8:05 to 8:15 P.M. Central War Time, a German short wave radio station read messages from ten Americans who are prisoners of war in Germany. A message to you from Robert Spahar read:
"Arrived safe in Germany as a prisoner"
It was announced that these men had recently been transferred from a camp in southern Germany to one in northern Germany.
I would be interested in knowing whether you have received any other reports.
John R. Fike

CHARLES P. FIKE
Attorney at Law

12020 Shamrock Plaza
Omaha, Nebraska 68154-3537
(402) 778-5016
(402) 778-5036 Fax
Email: charlesfike@msn.com

May 22, 2006

Lisa L. Spahr
301 North Beauregard St. #711
Alexandria, Virginia

> Re: WW II Letters

Dear Lisa:

I am writing in response to your recent letter concerning your WW II POW grandfather, and the letters received your great-grandmother regarding his status while imprisoned, which was gathered by short wave radio listeners.

Your letter was in reference to my father, John R. Fike (who died here in 1988). Your letter was very touching and uplifting, and we thank you for undertaking your project to contact the relatives of senders of the POW information.

I have shared your letter with a number of family members, including children and grandchildren (and am now sending copies to my two sisters), and all were very moved by it.

The radio that my Dad used is still in the family (one of my wife's nephews has it). The war days were the days before television, and we, like many others, would gather around the big radio in the living room in the evenings to listen to Jack Benny, Fibber McGee & Molly, Edgar Bergan & Charlie McCarthy, etc., and the serialized programs.

However, as you now have discovered, my Dad also listened to short wave, and discovered that the Germans were allowing American POWs to broadcast short messages home. My Dad took down the messages and the family information and attempted to get the information into the hands of the POW's family. He soon realized that very often this was the only information that the families had received.

On one occasion, the family address did not come through clearly, so Dad did the best he could, but it turned out not to be good enough. His letter bounced around for awhile, and I think it got into some "dead-end" -type Department of the Post Office.

The letter ultimately came into the hands of the FBI, who became suspicious that Dad might be a German spy. He received a call, and one summer's evening we were joined in the short wave listening by an Agent, who obviously discovered the true state of things.

Again, thanks for taking the time to try to contact the senders of the short wave information after all these years. You must be a pretty special person to do that, and you should know that all of us connected to my Dad appreciate your effort, and the good memories it has brought back.

Very truly yours,

Charles P. Fike

Charles P. Fike

CHAPTER 4

The Letters
Came in Droves

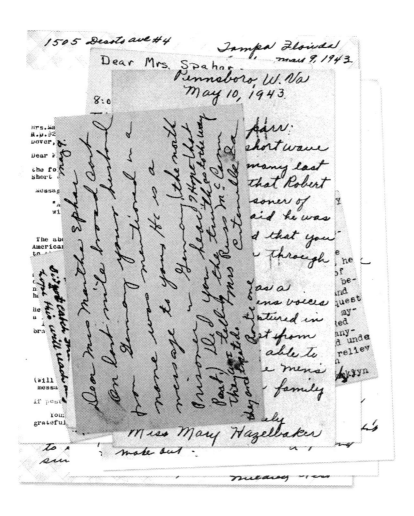

Shortly after May 10th, 1943, I believe my great-grandmother would have received her first message relay, from someone who identified himself or herself only as "a friend" from Frankfort, N.Y. This postcard was postmarked May 8th at 5:30 p.m. This author was one of several who chose to remain anonymous in their postcards and letters.

Dear friend,

Probably you've already received a message similar to this but I thought I'd inform you anyway. In listening to the shortwave Saturday evening I heard the following message addressed to you.

Arrived safe in Germany.

Signed Robert

I couldn't get the last name very well but I guess it started Mrcp ___ the rest I couldn't make out.

A friend

The next letter was from Sanford Lowe, New York City. Mr. Lowe noted that he had written 873 letters at the time he sent one to my great-grandmother. He also said that the postage had been donated by a grateful recipient of one of his previous letters.

In my research, I found an article that mentioned Mr. Lowe's large-scale message relay campaign.[6] In fact, the article stated that he had sent more than 10,379 letters to POW family members during the war.

---

6. Honoring those who listened—Captain George Duffy's POW Page. www.usmm.org/duffyhonoring.html.

Paul Kany, Johnstown, Pa., signed "your faithful servant" in his postcard to my great-grandmother. Mr. Kany also noted that my grandfather had arrived in Germany from Italy and reported fine health.

Irwin F. Bender of Oberlin, Pa. sent my great-grandmother a detailed letter about a radio message he had picked up "on 7-mega-cyles" regarding the capture of "our dear American boys" in Tunisia. Mr. Bender asked my great-grandmother if she might please "donate a stamp or so to keep up the good work of message relays." And because he had no way of knowing whether he had my great-grandmother's correct address, he included a message in case the postmaster opened the letter before relegating it to the dead-letter file: "Your kind cooperation in locating this boy's next-of-kin will be gratefully appreciated."

May 8, 1943

Mrs.Martha Spahr,
R.D.#2
Dover,Pa.

Dear Friend:-
                  This evening at 9:00 P.M. (E.W.T.)
the following message was read by the German announcer from
Short Wave Station DXP in Berlin,Germany on 7-megacycles:-

Message from Robert M. Spahr to Mrs.Martha Spahr:-

    "Arrived safely in Germany as a prisoner. Letter
    will follow later.
                    -Robert."

  The above was the 6th one of 10 messages read from our own dear
American boys who were captured in Tunisia and are now "in transit"
to the American War Prisoners' Camp "somewhere in southern Germany."
According to the German correspondent,this is a new camp with the
best of facilities. He said there are now more than 2,000 of our boys
already in the camp and more are arriving each day. When your loved
one gets to the camp, he will write to you,giving his prisoner's
number,the name of his camp and his barracks' number which you must
have in order to write to him.
  I have received a letter from Mrs.C.B.Hoenscheid of Davenport,Iowa.
Her boy's message was read on April 8th and on April 28th she received
a letter from him. Letter came via France.
  I trust this information will be of value to you and hope your
brave loved one keeps well and is returned safely to you.
                    Respectfully yours,
                                        Irwin F. Bender
                    Irwin F. Bender
                    124 N. 2nd Street
                    Oberlin,Pa.

(Will you please donate a stamp or so to keep up the good work of
 message relays?)

If postmaster for Dover opens this:-

    Your kind cooperation in locating this boy's next-of-kin will be
gratefully appreciated.
                    I.F.Bender.

Similarly, Mrs. Earl Seigle of Tyler, Texas went to great pains to contact my great-grandmother, sending her a letter by air-mail special delivery at the very high rate of 18 cents, with a notice on the envelope asking the postmaster to open the letter if necessary and to "make effort to contact party," because it involved a "radio message from American War Prisoner in Germany."

In a poignant letter, Edward D. Rapier of New Orleans sent my great-grandmother a brief notice that he had accidentally tuned in to a German broadcast and heard that Robert Spahr was safe in a prison camp, and asking that she please "excuse this stationery; it is all I have here." If Mr. Rapier had only known what a hero he was to the Spahr family.

> Mrs Martha Spahr
> RD # 2 Dover Pa
>
> By accident tuned my radio onto a German station and heard them say that ROBERT SPAHR is safe in a prison camp in southern Germany
>
> EDW. D. RAPIER
> 7640 JEANNETTE ST
> NEW ORLEANS LA
>
> Excuse this stationary it is all I have here

Letters from People Concerned About Their Own Servicemen

Mrs. Joseph Susan of McKeesport, Pa. reminded us that soldiers' families had a bond like no other. Unlike many of the other message-relayers, Mrs. Susan recalled that my grandfather ended his radio message by saying, "Love, Robert." She then added, "If this message helps to ease your mind and heart, then I am well repaid for I, too have a loved one in the service."

> 1019 Jenny Lind St.
> McKeesport, Pa.
> May 8, 1943
>
> Dear Mrs. Spahr,
>
> I just heard the following message read over the radio by shortwave from Germany between 9 – 9:15 tonight. It came from Robert Spahr and was directed to:
>
> Mrs. Martha Spahr
> R. D. #2
> Dover, Pa.
>
> Arrived safely in Germany as prisoner.
>
> Love
> Robert
>
> The announcer said tonight's messages were from soldiers who had been taken prisoners in Tunisia. They were at a camp in southern Germany, but have now been sent to a permanent camp in northern Germany.
>
> If this message helps to ease your mind and heart, then I am well repaid for I, too have a loved one in the service.
>
> Sincerely yours,
> Mrs. Joseph Susan

One of the most interesting messages came from Mrs. F. E. Keith of Parkersburg, W. Va., who advised my great-grandmother that she had heard the short-wave broadcast from Robert Spahr—and then went on to say that "Two weeks ago today, we received word in this same way that our own son Lewis is also a prisoner of Germany." Thus, Mrs. Keith apparently was so happy to receive word of her own son through the short-wave message relay "system" that she decided to join the network herself. Even though Mrs. Keith was unable to hear my great-grandmother's first name in the radio broadcast, she went ahead and sent a postcard addressed only to "Mrs. Spahr," and said that she was "hoping and praying that this will reach you,"— no doubt because she knew first-hand how important such a message could be to a mother.

In another fascinating message, Mrs. J. C. Bradford of Pennsboro, W. Va., wrote to say she heard the news of my grandfather being taken prisoner while she was listening to the radio in hopes of hearing news of her own brother-in-law. Mrs. Bradford may have been aware that people like my great-grandmother often received messages from multiple radio listeners; she closed by saying, "I am writing you on the chance that you may not have heard it before."

Like other activists in the message-relay system, Miss Flora Hill of Lewistown, Pa. said "I listen to the messages every night." After telling my great-grandmother that her son was safe, Miss Hill noted that her own sister had received such a message about her son, also a POW in Germany.

In my search for Miss Flora Hill, I received a letter from James and Kris Hill in Lewistown, who responded to my inquiry even though they did not know of a Flora Hill in their family. Nevertheless, they told me about James's father's service as a waist gunner in a B-17 "Flying Fortress" bomber. He was stationed in Mendlesohn, England, and flew 23 missions. As James recalled the stories, his father returned from each mission saying he had "only" a few holes in his wing. James lost his father to respiratory failure in 2005. He thanked me for my research on the message relay system, wished me the best, and said he would continue to ask relatives if they knew of a Flora Hill.

Dear Madam:—
I heard a message over the short-wave radio this evening shortly after nine which was directed to you. It came from Robt. M. Spahr who is evidently your son. The text of the message was: "Have arrived safely in Germany as a prisoner of war".
Robt.
I hope you are consoled by this message. I listen to the messages every night and my sister has received a similar message from her son who is also a German pris. of war.
Sincerely,
Miss Flora L. Hill

5/8/43.

Many of the messages sent to my great-grandmother are so sad and poignant, it is difficult not to cry as you read them. Margaret Fowler of Charlottesville, Va. wrote to tell my great-grandmother what she had heard of my grandfather, then went on to say, "My husband is a p. of w. of the Japanese, he was on Bataan. I would love to have someone send on to me a message from him." But Mrs. Fowler immediately returns her attention to my great-grandmother, noting that in his radio message, my grandfather promised to send his mother a letter. "I hope you receive your letter soon," Mrs. Fowler said in concluding her note.

Message Relay Templates

Herman Winkler of New York, N.Y. apparently sent a large number of message relays; in order to save time, he used a typed template rather than writing individual letters. But he hand-wrote the particular information about each soldier.

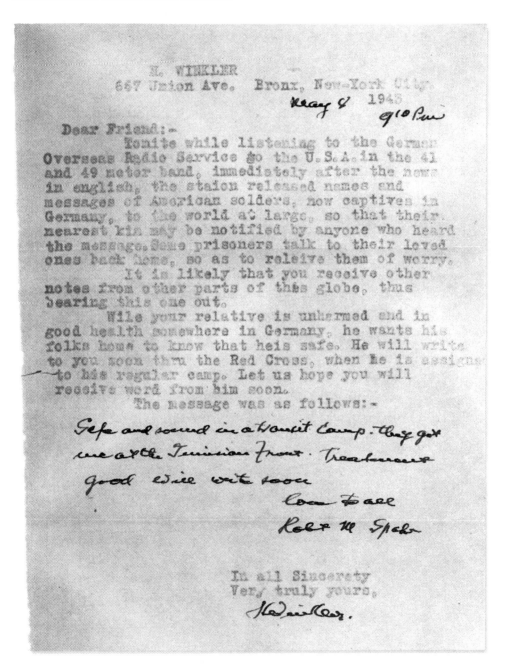

Another template message relay came in from Walter Duncan of Brooklyn, N.Y. Mr. Duncan, after describing the details of my grandfather's radio message, mentions that the radio reception was "very bad." This helps to explain why some of the relay messages are missing some of the details or have some of the information wrong. Mr. Duncan also apparently felt concern that some recipients of his messages might get their hopes too high about the fate of their loved ones. "This is not an official message as it was received via an enemy short wave station," he noted.

```
                                        WALTER DUNCAN
                                        I58 HICKS ST.,
                                        BROOKLYN, N.Y.

    Mrs. Martha Spahr.                  MAY. 9, I943.
    R.D· # 2
    Dover, Penn.


        My Dear Mrs. Spahr;
                        The following message was received by me via,
German short wave radio station from Berlin. Time received was I:I5 A.M.
The message is as follows :::
                " PRISONER OF WAR IN GERMANY "

            NAME :::::   ? SPAHR

            NUMBER :::   NONE

            ADDRESS ::   RURAL DELIVERY # 2 , DOVER, PENN.

            NOTIFY :::   MARTHA SPAHR.

            " ARRIVED ALL RIGHT IN GERMANY. I AM WELL. PLEASE DON'T WORRY.
            WILL WRITE AS SOON AS POSSIBLE. LOVE ."


        * * * * * ** ** * * * ** * * * * * * * * * * ** * ** *



                  ***********************
            NO OTHER MESSAGE WAS RECEIVED BY ME. RECEPTION VERY BAD.
            This is not an official message as it was received via
    an enemy short wave station.
                                        Sincerely yours,


                                        _____
                                        WALTER DUNCAN.
```

William Coonley of Troy, N.Y. developed an unusual template postcard for his message relays, which provides an insight into how the German broadcasts were organized. Apparently on some days, the German radio announcer would simply read a list of American prisoners' names. On other occasions, individualized messages from prisoners were read.

Dear Friend:

May 8, 1943. This evening at *9*. P. M. on the German short wave radio:

(1) An announcer read a list of American men held prisoners of war. The names were read without comment and no messages given. One of the names was

(2) An announcer read in English a list of names of American prisoners and gave a message from each. One was from

Robert M. Speake and it said "I am in Germany as prisoner of war and am safe." The announcer said the men had been brought from Italy to Germany and are now in camp in the northern part of the country

. . Message may not be word for word, but substantially as given above. Pardon possible errors or incomplete names, because it is sometimes hard to understand.

Very truly yours,

WILLIAM E. COONLEY,
499 Eighth Ave., Troy, N. Y.

Holding Out Hope Amid Suspicion

The Red Cross and other groups were heavily involved in ensuring that prisoners in World War II were afforded their rights under international conventions. But some of the letters in the message relay system show that there was concern about the treatment of American POWs by the Germans. Many of the letters to my great-grandmother state that my grandfather said he was "well," or "all right," and that he had "arrived safely." In the following letter, Mrs. Russ McCann wonders, "I hope that they are telling the truth as to the way they are treated."

A letter from Marguerite Costenbader of Washington, D.C. offered additional details about the German broadcasts, saying that American soldiers "were allowed to give their names and the address of some member of their family here in the States," and that "each boy requested that anyone hearing the broadcast please to notify the person named." I suspect that Miss Costenbader may have sent more than a few letters based on the broadcast she heard; her letter to my great-grandmother referred to a message from James C. Caraway, not Robert Spahr. I suppose she simply mixed up the names in sending letters to a number of people.

THE UNITED STATES FIELD ARTILLERY ASSOCIATION
Publishers of

The Field Artillery Journal

1218 CONNECTICUT AVENUE, WASHINGTON, D. C.

May 10, 1943

Mrs. Sphar
Dover
Pennsylvania

Dear Mrs. Sphar:

While dialing among the shortwave stations on our radio late Saturday night, my father accidently picked up a German broadcast from North Africa. During the program, American soldiers being held as prisoners of war were allowed to give their names and the address of some member of their family here in the States. Each boy requested that anyone hearing the broadcast please to notify the person named.

A "James C. Caraway" spoke and gave your name as his sister. At that time reception was not too clear, but we were able to understand that he had been captured in Tunisia but was not wounded. Perhaps, you too have heard the program or already been informed of it. There is no way to be sure that it was not purely propaganda and for that reason, I am very much interested in knowing if the above person is a member of your family.

Although the news carrys a certain sadness with it, if you can identify James Caraway, there is the knowledge that he is "somewhere" and a hope of reunion when all the horror of this war is past.

Cordially and sincerely,

Marguerite Costenbader

Marguerite Costenbader
512 Edgewood Street, N. E.
Washington, D. C.

"The FIELD ARTILLERY JOURNAL of today is the training regulations of tomorrow"

Walter Finke of Saginaw, Mich. provided a high level of detail in a two-page letter (on the next page) to my great-grandmother, one of the longest messages she received. Mr. Finke makes an almost desperate attempt to console my great-grandmother, saying, "I hope this will in some way relieve your anxiety in case you have not heard from him…. I am sure he is all right and hope that soon this war will be ended and he can give you his messages more direct." In fact, however, Mr. Finke's letter was dated May 8, 1943; the war was less than halfway over.

An anonymous letter (below) was received from New York, N.Y., signed, "A Loyal American."

Saginaw Mich
Saturday May 8, 1943

Mrs. Martha Spahr:-

Being a total stranger to you, this
letter may seem strange to you, but I
hope it will be welcome.

I was listening to my radio this evening
over short wave, and tuned in Germany, where
they were broadcasting in English. They gave a bit
war news which I listened to with a grain of
salt, and then they broadcast messages of
American prisoners of war.

A soldier by the name of ___ Spahr
was mentioned, (I could not understand the
first name) and he was sending a message
to you, saying "Arrived safely in
Germany as a prisoner."

Many other names and messages were

given but I just wrote this one down, with
the intention of writing to someone and telling them about it. You may have this
information already from the War Department

Other messages said that they were "well
and not to worry" also to contact the Red
Cross in regards to sending parcels, many
of them said address would be mailed soon.

I hope this will in some way relieve your
anxiety in case you have not heard from
him. I do not know whether he is your
son or husband, and would appreciate an
answer from you, letting me know if you
received this letter. I am sure he is all-
right and hope that soon this war will be
ended and he can give you his
messages more direct.

I hope you will answer and let me
know if you already had this message.
                Yours truly, Walter A. Finke
                1839 Arthur St.,
                Saginaw Mich

41

Prisoner Packages

John Kienitz of Brooklyn, N.Y. wrote to my great-grandmother to alert her of my grandfather's capture. Mr. Kienitz also noted that my grandfather promised to write as soon as possible. And he passed along advice he had heard about what prisoners hope most to receive from home: toothbrushes and underwear.

> 367-95th St., Brooklyn, N.Y
> May 9th, 1943
>
> Dear Madam: ·
>   In case you should have missed a mess-
> age to you by your son, which I by chance over-
> heard on the radio, I wish to advise you that he
> sends you and all his loved-ones his love; that he
> is in good health , and at present a prisoner of
> war, probably somewhere in Germany; that he is be-
> ing treated well; that you should not worry, and
> that he hopes to see you soon. The general request
> is to pass on these messages of which I avail my-
> self only too gladly. He will write through Red
> Cross as soon as possible.- If you send him any-
> thing, I understand, let it be toothbrush and unde
> wear, as general advice goes.- Hope to have reliev
> anxiety, with best wishes of an early re-union
>   John Kienitz
>   Brooklyn

Kathyleen Harper of Birmingham, Ala. provided a great deal of information she had learned about the types of food and other things that could be sent to prisoners. Miss Harper also showed a great deal of Southern charm, saying, "The minute you receive Robert's address, please send it to me as I have made arrangements to have a Bible sent to each boy. When you have time, I would love to hear all about your son; naturally I am interested after hearing his message."

May 10, 1943

Mrs. Martha Spahr,
R. F. D. #2,
Dover, Penna.

Dear Mrs. Spahr:

Saturday night I was listening to a Short Wave Broadcast from Germany and they gave the names of some American Prisoners and messages to their families. One was to you from your son, Robert. He said, "Arrived safe in Germany. Am well. Do not worry. Will write when I can."

When the Germans officially releases Robert's name to the United States Government, they will notify you that he is a prisoner of the Germans and will give you instructions how to write and send packages. The package cannot weigh over eleven pounds, must not contain anything that comes in metallic containers, such as tooth paste or shaving cream. Nothing that comes in cans, but pasteboard boxes and cellophane wrappers are all right. The boys have to wear khaki, so besure and get khaki socks. You can send a razor and blades, also cigarettes and smoking materials. Dehydrated foods do not weigh much and dried fruits are grand for them. A friend of mine sent powder milk and her son loves hot chocolate, so she mixed cocoa, powder milk and sugar, all he has to do is add the water and heat it. You cannot send literature, but you can write the publishers and they can send direct to the son. I do think the boys would enjoy, "Life," "Time," and the "Readers Digest." The minute you receives Robert's address, please send it to me as I have made arrangements to have a Bible sent to each boy.

When you have time, I would love to hear all about your son, naturally I am interested after hearing his message.

Very truly yours,

Kathyleen Harper

Kathyleen Harper
Tutwiler Hotel

Mrs. V. C. Clark writes that most prisoners ask for candy and cigarettes.

Dear Mrs. Spahr: May 8, 1943

            Your son Robert is a prisoner of
war in Germany,captured in Tunisia. I heard this
message tonight,on a short wave broadcast from
Germany. Your son is safe,in good health, and
says that he will write as soon as he can, and
asks you not to worry about him. Most of the
 messages ask that their parents or who ever is
 most cencerned get in touch with the Red Cross
 and send packages. They ask mostly for candy and
 cigarettes.
                Sincerely,
                        Mrs.V.C.Clark

An unusual message relay came from Mrs. Kenneth Ball of Erie, Pa. Rather than simply relaying all of the information she could remember from the broadcast, Mrs. Ball asked to be contacted if the recipient of her letter had a relative by the name of Spahr who was serving in the African campaign. I wonder whether Mrs. Ball was concerned about the wartime warnings that "loose lips sink ships," and thought that she should not share information about my grandfather's whereabouts until she had established a firm contact with one of his relatives.

In addition, the radio broadcast may have been garbled or full of static; Mrs. Ball's letter was addressed to Mrs. Martin Spahr, and refers to a soldier named Martin. But my great-grandmother received it nevertheless.

> 2110 E. 10th St., Erie, Pa.,
> May 4, 1943.
>
> Mrs. Martin Spahr
> Dover, Pa., Rd #2
>
> Dear Madam:
> If your husband or any relative by the name of Martin Spahr is a soldier in the African campaign would you please advise me, as I have a message of importance to you.
>
> Very Sincerely.
> Mrs. Kenneth Ball.

Mrs. F. G. Farrell, Cleveland, Ohio, wrote to my great-grand-mother as a POW mother herself (letter is on the next page). She received word of her son's imprisonment one week earlier via short-wave radio. She tells my great-grandmother that if the announcer was telling the truth, the prison camp is new and there is little reason to worry for their sons. She also gets his name incorrect, calling my grandfather "Paul."

Arthur Hensen of Ithaca, N.Y. was unable to hear my grandfather's name or other informa-tion, but he did hear my great-grandmother's name and address, and that was all he needed to send a message of good cheer to a worried mother.

May 9/1943

Dear Mrs. Spahn,

Last night over the German short wave radio I received a message from your son. There would a'l l long message but I couldn't get it. However is is a German prisoner safe and well in Germany I didn't get the name either but I did get your name & address.

Sincerely yours
Arthur R. Hensen

May 8 - 43
Cleve O.

Dear Mrs Sphar.

Last night while we were tuned in on the short wave broadcast from Germany we heard this message announced It was from your Son. The message read as follows.

Dear Mom.

Arived in Germany a prisoner. Am well and don't worry will write soon.
love
Paul.

I recived this same kind of messeage last Sted. and my son is also a prisoner of war in Germany. I do hope that this information will releave you of worries about your son as it has me.

The announcer gave all details about this new prisoner camp. and if it is all that he says it is don't worrie over your son.
I. Remain
Mrs F.J. Farkell
3034 Seymour ave
Cleve. O.

P.S. Please let me know if you received this messeage.

As I said earlier, I could only read a few of these letters at a time, because even though they were written from one stranger to another, *they are so intensely personal.* The letter on the next page, from Mrs. Alma Hodges of Rolla, Mo., is a great example: "If you get this letter I would like to have a line from you, as I am writing to several mothers for their sons and hope they gave their right names and addresses. You might have heard from him before now. But if you haven't, this will let you know he is still alive, and that means everything to you and family. Will close now. With best wishes for your son and all of you." Ms. Hodges also notes that a woman read my grandfather's name and family details. Other letters say that he gave the information himself.

Miss Mary Hazelbaker, Pennsboro, W. Va., said that the prisoners' voices were recorded and played via short-wave radio.

Pennsboro, W. Va
May 10, 1943.

Mrs. Martha Sparr:
I heard over short wave radio from Germany last Saturday night that Robert Sparr was a prisoner of war there. He said he was safe and well and that you could write to him through the Red Cross.
The broadcast was a recording of the mens voices when they were captured in Tunis and broadcast from Germany. I was able to hear several of the mens names and their family addresses.
Sincerely
Miss Mary Hazelbaker

1311 State St
Rolla Mo
May 9 - 43

Dear Mrs Spahr -

As I was listening to
My Radio last night I
heard A German Broadcast
And they were giving some
of the American Boys Names
that they Captured. And
they gave your sons Name
and your Name and Address
And ask if Any one heard
the Broadcast to try and
get in touch with you
so I am writing you. some
of the Boys talked themselves
And gave their own Names
& their home Address. I did

Not hear your son talk
A lady gave his Name -
As Robert - And gave your
Name & address. if you get
this letter I would like to have
A line from you. as I am
writing to several Mothers for
their sons and hope they gave
their right Names & addresses.
you might have heard from him
before Now. but if you haven't
this will let you know he is still
Alive and that means Every thing
to you and family. will close
Now. with best wishes for your
son and All of you.

Yours truly
Mrs Alma Hodges

49

Corporal Magdalene Hoffield, Pittsburgh, Pa., noted that prisoners wrote messages which were later relayed over the air by an announcer. Further, the corporal notes that her relaying messages have become another service delivered by the First Aid Ambulance Corps.

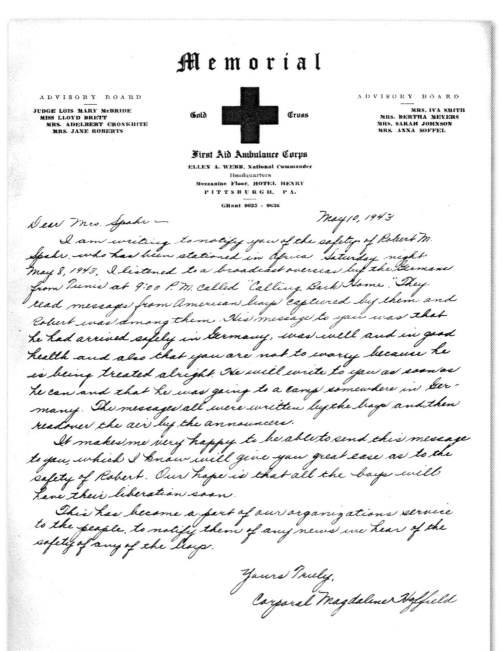

May 10, 1943

Dear Mrs. Spahr —

I am writing to notify you of the safety of Robert M. Spahr, who has been stationed in Africa. Saturday night May 8, 1943, I listened to a broadcast overseas by the Germans from Tunis at 9:00 P.M. called "Calling Back Home." They read messages from American boys captured by them and Robert was among them. His message to you was that he had arrived safely in Germany, was well and in good health and also that you are not to worry because he is being treated alright. He will write to you as soon as he can and that he was going to a camp somewhere in Germany. The messages all were written by the boys and then read over the air by the announcers.

It makes me very happy to be able to send this message to you, which I know will give you great ease as to the safety of Robert. Our hope is that all the boys will have their liberation soon.

This has become a part of our organizations service to the people, to notify them of any news we hear of the safety of any of the boys.

Yours Truly,

Corporal Magdalene Hoffield

Hazel Woodley, Somerville, Mass., noted the poor reception, static and difficult accent in the radio transmission.

```
                                    63 Willow Avenue
                                    Somerville, Mass.
                                    May 10, 1943



     Mrs. Martha Spahr
     R. D. #2
     Dover, Pa.

     Dear Mrs. Spahr:

          While listening to a short wave broadcast Saturday evening,

     a message came through from "a camp in Northern Germany" which is

     purported to be from your son.  The message is as follows:

                    "Arrived safely in Germany as a prisoner."

                    Signed Robert

     There may have been more to this message - I am not sure - for the

     static was bad, and the German accent isn't easy to understand.

     However, maybe you will receive a letter from someone else who

     heard it and you will have the whole story.  At least, I hope the

     above is encouraging news.

                    Very truly yours,

                    Hazel P. Woodley
```

Mrs. Jean Alvarez, Newark, N.J., mistakenly signed her own name "Mrs. Jean Spahr." The number of letters that relay messengers sent, the enormity of the task and the stress of a country being at war surely fostered a few mistakes in message relays here and there.

Newark N. J.
May 13, 1943

Dear Mrs Spahr:
          Heard over a
shortwave broadcast that Robert
Spahr is a prisoner of war in
Germany. Is in good health and
dont worry.

          Sincerely
          Mrs. Jean Spahr.

George Bigler, Camden, N.J., hopes that the message relay will be a cherished Mother's Day gift for my great-grandmother.

> Camden N.J.
> May 9-43
>
> On May 9th at 1.A.M. Berlin news radio announced Robert Spahew as a war prisoner. Following is a message he sent to you by radio
>
> I arrived safe and sound in Germany and am now at a camp there. Letter will follow. Ho not worry
>
> I hope you appreciate this bit of news I was able to get by short wave radio and send to you as a mothers day gift
> Yours Resp.
> Geo E Bigler
> 2628 Federal St
> Camden N.J.
>
> Please Ans.

Mildred West, Tampa, Fla., wrote the longest quoted transmission, apparently from my grandfather.

1505 Desoto ave #4

Tampa Florida
Sunday. May 9, 1943

Dear Mrs Spahr:-

Listening in on my short wave radio last night, I heard, with many others, a message broadcast from Berlin from your son. I didn't get his first name because of static conditions, but the message from him was:- Hello mom:- am now a prisoner of war. I was captured on the Tunisian front. and flown to Italy. I am now in Germany feeling fine, dont worry. I will write as soon as possible. You may contact me through the American Red Cross. Lose.

I have names and addresses of nearest kin of many others. They asked anyone who head the messages to get in touch with their families. I am writing others in hopes this news from their sons will ease to some extent the anxiety I am sure they have for them.

Best Regards
Mildred West

Mrs. F. H. Kahler, Bloomsburg, Pa., writes to my great-grandmother telling her when she can listen to future short-wave broadcasts to possibly hear my grandfather.

Dear Mrs. Spahr,   May 8th

while listening to short wave from Berlin tonite I heard the following message being sent to you from your son "Robert".

I have arrived safe in Germany as a prisoner of war. Please don't worry. — I hope you were lucky enough to have heard this broadcast. Please let me know. Try and listen to the short wave from Berlin May 10th, 11th and 12th as some of our boys are going to broadcast. I hope this card brings you some comfort in knowing that your son is well and safe.

Sincerely,
Mrs. F. H. Kahler
Light Street Road
Bloomsburg, Pa

Ted Wohlford, Wyulam, Ala., wrote a lengthy letter noting his message relay. He noted the pride that he felt by being able to relay this information and the belief that my great-grandmother would be relieved to know her son is alive.

May 8 - 1943

Mrs Martha Spahr
R.F.D. # 2
Dover Pa.

Dear Mrs Spahr,

I am taking the liberty of writing you these few lines with the hopes they will bring you a bit of good cheer, in so far as it concerns someone who is dear to you.

Tonight while listening to a broadcast direct from Berlin Germany, I heard a message from Robert M Spahr, saying that he was a prisoner of war, being taken by the Germans in Tunisia, he said for you not to worry about him, for he was well and fine, and was being treated o.k. He said he would write as soon as possible, and for you to give his regards to all his friends.

After receiving official notice from the Government which I take it you have, I feel sure that you will feel somewhat relieved over the situation after reading this, after all just knowing that he is still alive and is trying to get a message to you, must mean everything to you, and I am very proud that I can furnish you with this little message from him, for I know it will be greatly appreciated, and my hopes are that you hear direct from him in the near future, a long, long letter. My prayers are that God will watch over all our boys over there and bring them back home soon, victorious.

Sincerely yours

Ted Wohlford.
4913 - 7th Ave.,
Wylam Ala.

CHAPTER 5

THE SHORT–WAVE AMATEUR MONITORS CLUB

Active members As of Jan 1, 1944

BAUMGREEN, Ed., 20666 Sydenham Road, Shaker Heights, Ohio — Saturday
BARRY, Mrs. L.A., 660 Springdale Ave., East Orange, N.J. — Tuesday
BECK, Miss Tilda, 206 E. 56th St., Box 146, New York 26, N.Y. — Monday
BITTIN, Mr. Roger, Lakefield, Minn. — Wednesday
CARTWRIGHT, Mrs. Mary, 461 Eastland Ave., Akron 5, Ohio — Thursday
COOPER, Mrs. E.E., 135 E. Palm Road, Wildwood Crest, N.J. — Friday
DANNEMANN, Mr. F.N.C., 5615   6th Ave., Brooklyn 20, N.Y. — Friday
DELAPPE, Mrs. Walter, Eight Acres, Yaphank, L.I., N.Y. — Tuesday
DENSON, Otto E., 2515 D 6th Ave., N. Birmingham, Ala. — Monday
DULEY, Mrs. Edgar, Elizabeth, Pa. —
DUNCAN, Mr. Walter, 158 Hicks St., Brooklyn 2, N.Y. —
GAR FINKER, Mrs. Francis Woodbury Ave., RFD 2,Box 20, Huntington,L.I,N.Y. — Monday
GARRARD, Mrs. Charles E., Campton, Ky. — Tuesday
GEN, Mrs. Fred, Route 2-A, West Auburn, Maine — Thursday
GORDON, Mr. Alex E., English Hotel, Indianapolis 4, Ind/ — Saturday
GRUBBS, Mrs. Robert, Route 2, Box 89, Bessemer, Ala. — Wednesday
HAYNARD, Mr. Charles, 2934 Queen Ave., Dearborn, Michigan — Wednesday
HAZELBAKER, Miss Mary, Pennsboro, W.Va. — Saturday
JANKAUSKAS, Mr. Flavius, 4606 Chester Ave., Philadelphia, Pa. — Monday
KENNEDY, Mr. George, 16 Forest St., Montclair, N.J. — Thursday
LANCER, Miss Marion, Seneca Falls, N.Y. — Saturday
LEVENSON, Mr. L.I., 15 N.St.Katherine Place, Atlantic City,N.J. — Friday
LEVINS, Mr. J. 150 Winthrop St., Brooklyn 35, N.A.Y. — Friday
LOWE, Mr. Sanford, 222 West 77th St., Apt. 1125, New York 34, N.Y. — Thursday
McLAUGHLIN, Rev. W.G., St. Michaels, Montgomery, Indiana — Wednesday
MILLER, Miss C.L. 13285 Marlowe, Detroit 27, Mich. — Wednesday
MOORE, Mrs. H.E., 1153 Martine Ave., Plainfield, N.J. — Saturday
MOORE, Ralph, 6703 Grandville, Detroit 10, Mich. — Friday
MULLER, Mrs. L. F., 36 Valleywood Road, Cos Cob, Conn. — Wednesday
OLSON, Mrs. B. C., 416 Witwer St., North Canton, Ohio — Saturday
ORIOLO, Nicholas, 1127   51st St., North Bergen, N.J. —
PELTON, Mrs. K.R.,314 Hyslip Ave., Westfield, N.J. — Saturday
PICKETT, Mr. Robert, 517 Longview Ave., Roanoke, Va. — Friday
PROPST, Mr. David, Black Mountain, N. Car. — Tuesday
SCHUM, Mr. LeRoy, 125 Belvedere Ave., Reading, Pa., — Tuesday
SHELTON, Mr. W. V., Box 59, Louisburg, N.Car. — Thursday
SHONTING, Martin G., 908 West Mnoe St., Troy, Ohio — Saturday
SKILTON, Mr. and Mrs. C.P., 150 Salem Ave., Carbondale, Penna. — Friday
TANCREE, Mrs. Carl, 512 West 23rd St., Erie, Penna. — Thursday
TAYLOR, Mr. Curtis, 107 Columbia St., Utica 2, N.Y. — Wednesday
WARREN, Roger E., 213 N. Aurora St., Ithaca, N.Y. — Saturday
WASHIL, Mr. J. Lee J., 333 West 76th St., New York, N.Y. — Monday
WATKINS, Morris, Box 42, Ulster, Penna. — Tuesday
WHITE, Mrs. Newton, Route 5, Bloomsburg, Penna. — Monday
WITTFEN, Russell, 50 Maiden Lane, New York 7, N.Y. — Thursday
YANT, Mrs. Don, 1175 Hazel Ave., Lima, Ohio — Tuesday
ZALESKI, Robert, 19 East Somerset St., Philadelphia 34, Pa. — Thursday.

Mr. J. Lee Washile, Madonna Book Sergice, Moscow, Penna.
M. Newton White, Route 5, Bloomsburg, Penna.
M. Don Yant, 1175 Hazel Ave., Lima, Ohio
Mr. Robert Zaleski, 19 E. Somerset St., Philadelphia 34 Penna.

Mr. Chauncey G. Gray, 100 Grams St., #3, Dayton, Ohio
Mr. Martin G. Shonting, 908 W. Bass St., Troy, Ohio.

SWAM roster, 1944

n my efforts to reach out to the wonderful souls who contacted by great-grandmother more than 60 years ago, I found one who introduced me to large-scale, organized effort by amateur radio listeners and operators to keep POW families informed.

Flavius Jankauskas of Philadelphia was 16 years of age when he wrote to "Miss Spahr" on May 9, 1943.

Flavius Jankauskas and his Howard 430 radio, 1942

Getting Organized—
"So No POW Family Would Go Without Notice"

During the 1930s, I developed a keen interest in amateur radio. I purchased the radio in this photograph [on previous page], a Howard 430, from the nickels and dimes I earned on my Liberty Magazine route.

In 1940, I diligently studied the Morse code, the technical radio knowledge of that time, and the rules and regulations in effect, and took the examination for a radio license by the Federal Communications Commission. I was assigned the call letters W3JAK, which I still use today. In 1940, we were banned from communicating with foreign countries. When December 7, 1941 happened, all "hamming" was banned for the duration. However, I continued to monitor and listen to short-wave stations, such as the BBC from London, Berlin Radio, and programs from other capital cities, listening to reports of the war's progress from my home in Philadelphia, Pa. At U.S. broadcast radio stations, many engineers were called into the service and I worked as a replacement at one of these stations.

It was during the time of listening on short-wave that I heard the POW messages over Berlin Radio and started sending notices to families of the POWs, often receiving a response of gratitude for the news.

In mid-1943, more than 45 listeners, including myself, were organized by a Mrs. Don Yant in Ohio into a group known as Short-Wave Amateur Monitors (SWAM). Mrs. Yant assigned several of us to each night of the week to monitor the enemy radio stations so that no POW family would go without notice. Mrs. Yant also shared the latest in radio news, techniques, and member news via monthly newsletters.

Following in the steps of the servicemen I was listening for, in April 1944, at the age of 17, I joined the Merchant Marine and started sailing ships for the war effort.

Flavius Jankauskas

Mr. Jankauskas was on my list, and I sent a letter trying to locate him. I found a listing for a man with the last name Jankauskas in Pennsylvania, and I figured that with such a unique name, I might have some luck with this one. My luck was better than expected, although it surfaced in an unusual way.

I was on a business trip when my cell phone rang. I excused myself from a meeting and took the call. It was from a gentleman, Mr. Jankauskas, in the Philadelphia area. He received my letter and wanted to touch base. He was not the Mr. Jankauskas whom I sought, nor did he know of him. However, he said he was touched by my mission to find Flavius and wanted to tell me he would keep his ears open. He did more than that; he completed his own Internet search and called me a few days later with a telephone number and address that he thought might be the Flavius whom I had been seeking. He was right. I found the one and only Flavius Jankauskas one evening via telephone.

Mr. Jankauskas told me that he had sent 50 to 100 postcards to POW families before joining the service himself in 1944 as a merchant marine, headed to the Persian Gulf.

Short-Wave Amateur Monitors Club

Mr. Jankauskas and I had several telephone conversations and much email correspondence, and he told me about the Short-Wave Amateur Monitors club (SWAM), organized by Mrs. Ruby Yant of Lima, Ohio. Mrs. Yant organized amateur radio operators and listeners to monitor the enemy broadcasts on specific nights of the week, to ensure that no POW's message would be missed, and that all POW families would receive word about their loved ones. The postcard on the next page was sent to amateur radio operators on July 1, 1943.

Mrs. Yant's resourcefulness paid off. The program was a success and the list of SWAM club members continued to rise. On the next page is a sample of the near-50 members and their assigned nights to listen and report to POW families. Of course the list includes Flavius Jankauskas.

Mrs. Yant frequently reached out to the SWAM members with updates. Even reading her simple bulletin, one can see why her

Dear Fellow Short Wave Fan: Let's Organize!
Thru' the kindness of Mr. Lowell Walker, I have the
names of 27 of you who are sending out messages and notices.
We know there are many more of us. Could we organize and ten
of us send out messages one night and ten the next, etc.?
If we can round up 60 of us, we would have ten for each night
in the week; if more we can divide it equally among us. I am
sure if we are no less then ten, we could get the messages
across alright. What do you think about it? Let me hear
from you. If you are interested, state the night you would
be most apt to be at home listening.
                                        Sincerely,
                                        Mrs Don Yant

        Mrs. Don Yant, 1175 Hazel Ave., Lima, Ohio

SWAM roster, 1944

Active members As of Jan 1, 1944

BAMBERGER, Ed., 20855 Sydenham Road, Shaker Heights, Ohio	Saturday
BARRY, Mrs. L. A., 650 Springdale Ave., East Orange, N.J.	Tuesday
BECK, Miss Tilde, 206 E. 86th St., Box 146, New York 28, N.Y.	Monday
BETTIN, Mr. Roger, Lakefield, Minn.	Wednesday
CARTWRIGHT, Mrs. Mary, 461 Eastland Ave., Akron 5, Ohio	Thursday
COOPER, Mrs. K.E., 125 E. Palm Road, Wildwood Crest, N.J.	Friday
DANNEMANN, Mr. F.W.C., 5615 6th Ave., Brooklyn 20, N.Y.	Friday
DELAPPE, Mrs. Walter, Eight Acres, Yaphank, L.I., N.Y.	Friday
DENSON, Otto K., 2515 D 6th Ave., N. Birmingham, Ala.	Tuesday
DUDLEY, Mrs. Edgar, Elizabeth, Pa.	Monday
DUNCAN, Mr. Walter, 158 Hicks St., Brooklyn 2, N.Y.	Wednesday
MRS FINGER, Mrs. Francis Woodbury Ave., RFD 2,Box 20, Huntington,L.I.N.Y.	
HUBBARD, Mrs. Charles K., Campton, Ky.	Monday
OVEN, Mrs. Fred, Route 2-A, West Auburn, Maine	Tuesday
GORDON, Mr. Alex K., English Hotel, Indianapolis 4, Ind/	Thursday
GRUBBS, Mrs. Robert, Route 2, Box 85, Bessemer, Ala.	Saturday
HAYWARD, Mr. Charles, 2934 Queen Ave., Dearborn, Michigan	Wednesday
HAZELBAKER, Miss Mary, Pennsboro, W. Va.	Wednesday
JANKAUSKAS, Mr. Flavius, 4605 Chester Ave., Philadelphia, Pa.	Saturday
KENNEDY, Mr. George, 16 Forest St., Montclair, N.J.	Monday
LANGER, Miss Marion, Seneca Falls, N.Y.	Thursday
LEVENSON, Mr. L.I., 15 N.St.Katherine Place, Atlantic City,N.J.	Saturday
LEVINS, Mr. J. 150 Winthrop St., Brooklyn 25, N.Y.	Friday
LOWE, Mr. Sanford, 222 West 77th St., Apt. 1125, New York 24, N.Y.	Friday
MCLAUGHLIN, Rev. W.G., St. Michaels, Montgomery, Indiana	Thursday
MILLER, Miss C.L. 13225 Marlowe, Detroit 27, Mich.	Wednesday
MOORE, Mrs. H.H., 1163 Martine Ave., Plainfield, N.J.	Wednesday
MOORE, Ralph, 6703 Grandville, Detroit 10, Mich.	Saturday
MULLER, Mrs. L. F., 36 Valleywood Road, Cos Cob, Conn.	Friday
OLSON, Mrs. B. C., 416 Witwer St., North Canton, Ohio	Wednesday
ORIOLO, Nicholas, 1127 51st St., North Bergen, N.J.	Saturday
PELTON, Mrs. K.R., 314 Hyslip Ave., Westfield, N.J.	
PICKETT, Mr. Robert, 517 Longview Ave., Roanoke, Va.	Saturday
PROPST, Mr. David, Black Mountain, N. Car.	Friday
SCHUM, Mr. LeRoy, 125 Belvedere Ave., Reading, Pa.,	Tuesday
SHELTON, Mr. W. F., Box 59, Louisburg, N.Car.	Tuesday
SHONTING, Martin G., 908 West Race St., Troy, Ohio	Thursday
SKILTON, Mr. and Mrs. C.P., 160 Salem Ave., Carbondale, Penna.	Saturday
LADAGENNE, Mrs. Carl, 812 West 23rd St., Erie, Penna.	Friday
TAYLOR, Mr. Curtis, 107 Columbia St., Utica 2, N.Y.	Thursday
WARREN, Roger B., 213 N. Aurora St., Ithaca, N.Y.	Saturday
WASHILA, Mr. J. Leo J., 333 West 76th St., New York, N.Y.	Monday
WATKINS, Morris, Box 42, Ulster, Penna.	Tuesday
WHITE, Mrs. Newton, Route 5, Bloomsburg, Penna.	Monday
WITTPENN, Russell, 50 Maiden Lane, New York 7, N.Y.	Thursday
YANT, Mrs. Don, 1175 Hazel Ave., Lima, Ohio	Tuesday
ZALESKI, Robert, 19 East Somerset St., Philadelphia 34, Pa.	Thursday.

Mr. Roger B. Warren, 213 North Aurora St., Ithaca,   N.Y.
Mr. J. Leo Washile, Madonna Book Service, Moscow, Penna.
Mr. Newton White, Route 5, Bloomsburg, Penna.
M.. Don Yant, 1175 Hazel Ave., Lima, Ohio
Mr. Robert Zaleski, 19 E. Somerset St., Philadelphia 34, Penna.

Mr. Chauncey G. Gray, 100 Crane St.,#3, Dayton,   Ohio
Mr. Martin G. Shonting, 908 W. Race St., Troy, Ohio.

SWAM program was such a success—she had the perfect combination of friendliness, can-do spirit, upbeat attitude, and resourcefulness about technical problems to inspire her troops. And she was funny! I'm tempted to quote from this bulletin, but a few quotations could

Short Wave Amateur Monitors Club
March 1, 1944   Bulletin No. 8

Hello again, Monitors:
    I am so happy to welcome six new members to our club. Mr. Claud Daily, 809 Cherry St., New Albany, Ind.; Mrs. Rose Gilli, Willoughby, Ohio; Mrs. George Lande, One Tenniss Court, Brooklyn 26, N.Y.; Mrs. Jack Thompson, RR1, Monangahala, Pa., and Mr. and Mrs. Livingston, 127 Woodbine Ave., Rochester 11, N.Y., and I also want to welcome Mrs. Pelton and Mrs. Finger as new members and Mrs. Allaway is back with us, being fortunate enough to get her radio fixed.

                    RADIO   SECTION
    Mr. C. Daily has a 9 tube Silvertone and a 9 tube Philco. He sent 126 messages from Saturday to Saturday, the week of Feb. 12th! The Livingstons have a professional Short Wave Radio.   Mr. Moore of Detroit gave these details on the Japanese broadcasts which several have asked for; 6:15 and 7:15 P.M.E.W.T., on 9.600 and 11.800 megs.   At 2:15 and 1:15 A.M. C.W.T., they repeat the same ones.   Mr. Jankauskas has offered us a service and I shall quote from his letter "Since almost everybody has been having trouble with reception, I would like to suggest that as most of us are using indoor aerials or loops built in the Radio, an outdoor aerial of fairly good size would, in practically all cases, bring reception up. If it is felt worth while, I would be glad to send data on right lengths, etc, on aerials for best possible reception".   I, for one, am certainly going to make use of this service!   Now something else about reception-a news commentator last week said the Allies have, for the past several months, carried in their planes and dropped over Germany, metal flutters.   These are strips of cardboard covered with tin foil and as they flutter thru' the air they play the dickens with reception.   They mentioned that Germany was just starting to use them.   Do you suppose that is our nasty interference?   How about it, Mr. Lowe?   Now, speaking of reception again-Let's give a one, two, three cheer to Mrs. H.H.Moore-she sent 502 messages in January!

                    NEWSBITS
    Mrs. Grubbs has been laid up with a broken arm!   Mrs. Lande's husband is in the service.   Mrs. Gabbard's son is on the Destroyer "Sigsbee".   Know anyone on that ship?   If you do write Mrs. Gabbard.   Miss Beck returns all money sent her with the suggestion that the War Prisoners Aid is grateful for any small donation.   And Mrs. Buchmaster called me and wanted to donate $5.00 to S.W.A.M. for the many cards and letters she received from the members.   I explained about our constitution and she said she would give the money to the Red Cross in our behalf.   I know that makes us all proud as we can feel we had a hand in doing something for the boys.   Mr. Moore thinks the convention should be in Tokyo instead of Berlin!   He also sent me a complete list of the Japanese camps.   If anyone would like this list, just write me.   Mr. Denson would like to hear from some of you.   He is our blind member in Birmingham.   Mr. Propst leaves soon for the Navy.   Would be funny if one of these bulletins turned up in Borneo someday.

SWAM Bulletin, March 1, 1944
(ON THIS AND FACING PAGES)

never capture Mrs. Yant's wonderful style. Read the whole newsletter
yourself.

Mrs. Yant highlights the commitment of the SWAM members in
the newsletter. Some of the members, individually, had written more

GENERAL   INFORMATION

Mrs. Bean received 50 cards. I believe that shows many people, like me, are
getting the names in the mornings and can't at night. Did you know Germany has the
same newscasts and names at 9:30 a.m. on Sundays? I didn't until Mr. Duncan mention
ed it. I'm running into a snag on pins and dies because of metals, I am sure I
can have more to report next month. Look for Mr. Gordon's picture in March Popular
Mechanics and February Radio News! A cellebrity, by heck! He is a fine booster
for our club! Speaking of pictures-where are they? Please don't keep them over
two days as that would mean only 15 could see them a month and four months for them
to get clear around. So please hurry them along! Mr. Zaleski sent me another
clipping about Miss Wainwright. She is still doing her dirty work! She notified
a girl who was to be married soon and her sweetheart was coming home on a ship and
went down. Miss W. called the girl and told her he was safe. It was false. The
comments on Miss W. in the clipping were "the voice on the wire was a woman's; it
was calm and refined; and there was a background of sound as tho' the speaker were
talking from an office where a number of people were working and talking." Parents
are making fine comments about S.W.A.M! Now take your lists of missing boys, start
with Dec. and run a line thru' these names as having been heard-McFadien, Tew,
Vonseggern,Guidaitis,Ballerino,Boudreau,Brubaker,Gallagher,Hawkins,Hazelton,
Jarosynski,Jackson,Keim,Larson,McKeegan,Wesner,Wright. Mr. Lowe has passed the
5000 mark and Mr. Dannemann has sent 3000. Rev. McLaughlin says the wave lengths
seem to waver so much and that in the evenings the only place to get the messages
is in the 7 meg. band. Oh, yes, and the small paper withths "Too Late to Classify"
for last time is included in this list, so destroy the small paper. Mrs. H. H. Moore
sent along a humorous but pathetic story-a mother couldn't wait for her Red Cross
instructions to write to her son so she addressed a letter to the Censor of the
largest air camp in Germany thinking the Censor would know her son.If this bulletin
costs 6¢ to send, I may type up a list of boys and send in the middle of the month.
That way you would have the addresses sooner and it would cost the same. As soon
as you get some missing boys send them along and if there are enough to compile,
look for a list in the middle of the month. Don said,"Don't you know how to start
a paragraph". I hope you all know I run it all together to save space and therefore money. If I started a new paragraph each time, it would take another stencil.
Mr. Skilton wrote a beautiful poem entitled "Missing in Action" and I want you all
to have it as soon as I can have room for it. Mrs. Skilton has another slogan for
us too- " Service With Altrustic Motives" You can't beat the Skiltons!
My first crocus is up so

Happy Springtime!   Ruby

than 1,000 postcards and letters to POW families. Earlier in this book I mentioned Mr. Sandord Lowe who sent a letter to my family as well as to others, I had discovered in my research. Mr. Lowe was a SWAM member and Mrs. Yant notes in her newsletter that he surpassed the "5,000-sent" mark! One member sent more than 126 in one week, and another sent 502 in January alone. Mrs. Yant alludes to SWAM members not accepting contributions from POW families in return for their hard work. Instead, SWAM asked that donors send their money to other organizations committed to helping the war effort and caring for veterans. The newsletters also provided an outlet for SWAM members to discuss radio technology and practices, member news, and war updates. The members were often praised and thanked by many POW families. One grateful person suggested that SWAM also stood for "Service With Altruistic Motives." I wholeheartedly echo that sentiment.

Radio Operators Today

Mr. Jankauskas informed me that there are 600,000 ham radio operators today (versus the 51,000 in 1939[7]) in the United States and more than 1.5 million worldwide. He still spends much of his time talking with people all over the world via his radio.

Flavius Jankauskas' call letters postcard

7. 50 Years of the American Radio Relay League (1965)
www.n4mw.com/ARRL.

CHAPTER 6

ROBERT SPAHR'S LEGACY

Kathryn and Robert Spahr (my grandmother
and grandfather) upon his return from WWII

R obert reentered the United States in May 1945 and was assigned to the Headquarters Detachment Separation Center. He requested a dependency discharge from the Army on August 9, 1945, as his mother was partially paralyzed from a stroke that occurred during the war and needed greater support from him. His four brothers remained in the Army. My great-grandmother passed on shortly thereafter.

As Great Aunt Marty told the story of Robert's return from the war, it was rather solemn. He had nowhere to go upon his return, so he went to her house. She offered him a bedroom upstairs, but he said he'd prefer to sleep on the downstairs floor. She never asked why, but let him do as he pleased. He was her hero. Whatever effects the war may have had on him, he never complained, never felt that he was owed anything. He simply moved on with his life, striving for the opportunities and success his father had intended for him to have.

Shortly after my grandfather's return from the war, he married my grandmother, Kathryn Marie Myers. He and Kathryn had four children: Robert Eugene, Charles Leroy, Beverly Ann (my mother), and Ida May. He spent the next 23 years in the petroleum business. He was very successful. Everyone in town always said the most kind things about my grandfather when they realized who I was. He was known to be a talkative man, never shying away from talking with a stranger. (We often joke that my Uncle Charlie inherited this trait from his father.) He was hardworking and dedicated to his family, his community and his country. Robert retired from

Kathryn and Robert Spahr

the petroleum business and began working for Standard Concrete Company of York, Pa., where my Uncle Charlie still works to this day. I am my grandfather's only grandchild.

Our family lost Robert in 1984. He was 68. His spirit lives on with us in each day.

On November 7, 1998, our hometown of Wellsville, Pa., erected a "Roll of Honor" plaque to commemorate the service of our World War II veterans. The Spahr brothers, along with the names of more than 250 of their comrades, can be found on the plaque.

Let us never forget our heroes. And let us acknowledge the unsung heroes who faithfully tuned in enemy short-wave radio broadcasts more than 60 years ago to learn about our boys' fates and to relay information to their grateful family members.

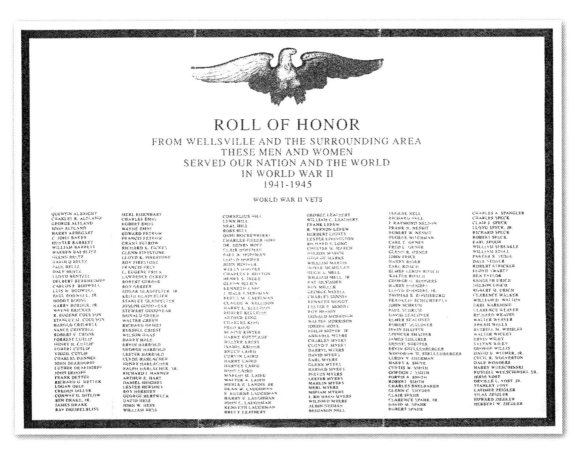

WWII Roll of Honor Plaque, Wellsville, Pa.

IF YOU HAVE BEEN MOVED BY THIS STORY—
the compassion of strangers—I encourage you to write your
own postcard or letter to someone today. This person could
be a military person serving far away from home, a stranger
you've heard about doing a good deed somewhere, or simply
reaching out to a long-lost friend. The art of letter writing is
becoming extinct with the age of email and one-liners via
chat lines. Surely we realize we are missing something in
those communications—something wonderful, personal
and close.

I encourage you to go into your attics, basements and
other storage places where you have items that have fallen
far from your mind. Revisit the treasures of generations past.
Talk with your family members about the people you've
loved and lost. Preserve your own history.

I am looking forward to my own journey continuing in
this area. I anticipate that I'll begin receiving word from so
many others who have found what I have, what I've written
about here. You may find that this book is only the beginning. I invite you to keep watching for our next adventure.

Lisa L. Spahr

About the
Author

LISA SPAHR is an investigative psychologist who owns a life
coaching and consulting business. Ms. Spahr has worked in the area
of behavioral health, delivering mental health and counseling ser-
vices to various populations over the years. In addition she has an
extensive history in the field of research for universities and private
organizations, focusing on law and psychiatry research, military
applications, and policing operations and tactics. Examples of her
work include examining the construct of psychopathy in prisoner
and juvenile offender populations, designing military exercises and
scenarios for technology evaluations, and creating guidelines for
suicide bomb response for police officers in the United States.

Ms. Spahr's respect for veterans—which started with her respect
for her grandfather and his brothers—led her to work for the American Legion's Washington D.C. office for several years as a researcher
and advocate examining issues related to the Gulf and Vietnam
conflicts.

Ms. Spahr was born in York, Pa. At the age of 19 she began moving around the world every few years. Her work has taken her to live
in Washington D.C. several times, but
she continues to return to the home she
has made for herself in Pittsburgh. Ms.
Spahr received her bachelor of arts degree
in psychology from Temple University
in Philadelphia and Rome, Italy and her
master's of science degree in investigative
psychology from the University of Liver-
pool in England.

Her hobbies include traveling, working on her Victorian home, and hiking
with her favorite pals, Syrah Jayne—
an Airedale mix—and Louie B—an
American Bulldog/Staffordshire mix.

Reach the author via www.lisaspahr.com.

About the
Editor and Contributors

Austin Camacho was born in New York City but grew up in Saratoga Springs, N.Y. He enlisted in the Army as a weapons repairman but soon moved into a more appropriate field as a broadcast journalist. During his thirteen years as a soldier, Austin lived in Missouri, California, Maryland, Georgia and Belgium. He also spent a couple of exciting weeks in Israel during Desert Storm, covering the action with the Patriot missile crews and capturing scud showers on videotape. He rose to the rank of Sergeant First Class. And in his spare moments, he began writing adventure and mystery novels set in some of the exotic places he'd visited.

After leaving the Army in 1996 he continued writing military news for the Defense Department as a civilian, frequently serving as on-air anchor for the American Forces Information Service. Today he does public affairs work for the DoD agency charged with providing health care to service members, retirees and their families. He has settled in northern Virginia with his wife Denise. For more information on Austin visit www.ascamacho.com.

Morton Bardfield developed an early interest in radio, and at age 16 when World War II ended, he received his amateur radio license. At age 17 he enlisted as a radioman private in the Massachusetts National Guard. He rose through the ranks to Lieutenant Colonel in the U.S. Army Reserve. During that time he served as a military aide to the Governor of Massachusetts and in various other posts, and also provided technical assistance in the communications and security fields. Lt. Col. Bardfield served 12 years as chief of security and communications for Suffolk County, Mass., and in several other government agencies. He is the founder and chief executive officer of E. Caribbean Cellular Telephone Network Company, and Comm-Systems Ltd. His businesses operate in Boston and St. Maarten. He and his wife, Claire, reside in Brookline, Mass., and their three children are involved in the family businesses.

CRAIG FISCHER is a Washington, D.C.-based writer and editor with 30 years of experience covering news and policy issues in the areas of criminal justice, government-funded science programs, airline safety, drug abuse, organized labor, and other matters. He holds a bachelor's degree in journalism from the University of Illinois. His father, James D. Fischer, joined the U.S. Army in 1944 at the age of 17, immediately following his high school graduation, and served as a lieutenant in Germany in 1945–46 after completing officer training.

FLAVIUS JANKAUSKAS is a short-wave radio operator and hobbyist who was closely related to the U.S. military in the post-WWII years. His first sea trip as a Merchant Marine, Radio Officer, was in 1944. He delivered military equipment all around the world during his years of service. He recalls hearing news of D-Day over BBC while in Bahrain. He heard about the Hiroshima and Nagasaki bombings while in mid-Pacific on the radio. Mr. Jankauskas spent 1952-54 residing in Stuttgart, Germany and was a student at Musik Akademie. He married while living abroad. He served as a Technical Representative in the U.S. Air Force, 1958–61, with the Military Field Service Division in Florida and Alabama. He retired in 1982. FWE. He resides in Pennsylvania with his companion.

JOHN F. SOMMER, JR. is the Executive Director of The American Legion National Headquarters Washington Office. He is responsible for overseeing the activities of the nation's largest veterans' organization in its dealings with The White House, Congress, and federal agencies such as the Departments of Veterans Affairs, Defense and State. Born in Columbus, Ohio, Mr. Sommer was educated in Grove City public schools. He graduated from Franklin University in Columbus with a B.S. in Business Administration in 1972. He has attended Bowling Green State University and the University of Michigan's Business School. Mr. Sommer's service as a U.S. Army combat medic included a tour of duty in Vietnam with the 4th Infantry Division where he was a Senior Company Medic and the NCO-in-charge of a battalion aid station. His service awards include the Bronze Star

Medal with "V" device, Army Commendation Medal, Combat Medical Badge, and Republic of Vietnam Gallantry Cross with Palm. Since 1991 Mr. Sommer has traveled to Vietnam numerous times and met with officials in other Southeast Asia countries regarding missing American servicemen. He has represented The American Legion on presidential delegations to Vietnam, Laos and Cambodia. The Sommer family resides in Annandale, Va.

DAVE WILLIAMS is a freelance graphic designer who works on print projects in the fields of criminal justice, civil engineering, health advocacy and home improvement, to name a few. He is very proud of the contributions his grandfather made in the service as a U.S. Marine in the Pacific Theater during World War II. He lives in Maryland with his wife and two daughters, and he can be reached at davewilliams@starpower.net.

PERMISSION AND ATTRIBUTIONS

The author has attempted to identify and locate the copyright owners of the letters and related material included in this edition of *World War II Radio Heroes Letters of Compassion*. Grateful acknowledgement is made to individuals who have kindly granted permission for the use of their materials in this edition of *World War II Radio Heroes Letters of Compassion*. If there are instances where proper credit is not given, the author will gladly make necessary corrections in subsequent printings.

PHOTOS/IMAGES

Page | Detail

1 | Hymn and Prayer Book, War Prisoner's Aid Y.M.C.A.

3 | German Phrase Book, United States Army.

7 | Spahr Family Photograph, Spahr Family Collection. Published with permission from Ida M. Spahr.

9 | Robert Spahr's Selective Service Card, Spahr Family Collection. Published with permission from Ida M. Spahr.

9 | War Department Telegram, Spahr Family Collection. Published with permission from Ida M. Spahr.

10 & 11 | Robert Spahr's Log from Prison Camp, Spahr Family Collection. Published with permission from Ida M. Spahr.

57 & 61 | SWAM Roster, Flavius Jankauskas Collection. Published with permission from Flavius Jankauskas.

58 | Flavius Jankauskas 1942, Flavius Jankauskas Collection. Published with permission from Flavius Jankauskas.

62 & 63 | SWAM Bulletin No. 8, Flavius Jankauskas Collection. Published with permission from Flavius Jankauskas.

64 | Flavius Jankauskas Call Card, Flavius Jankauskas Collection. Published with permission from Flavius Jankauskas.

65 | Spahr Family Photograph, Spahr Family Collection. Published with permission from Ida M. Spahr.

66 | Spahr Family Photograph, Spahr Family Collection. Published with permission from Ida M. Spahr.

67 | Roll of Honor, Wellsville Pa.

POSTCARDS/LETTERS

Page | From | To | Date

12 | Kathryn Myers | Robert Spahr | July 31, 1943. Published with permission from Ida Spahr

21 | John R. Fike | Martha Spahr | May 9, 1943. Published with permission from Charles P. Fike

22 | Charles P. Fike | Lisa Spahr | May 22, 2006 | Published with permission from Charles P. Fike

24 | Unknown | Martha Spahr | May 1943

25 | Sanford Lowe | Martha Spahr | May 1943

26 | Paul Kany | Martha Spahr | May 9, 1943

27 | Irwin F. Bender | Martha Spahr | May 8, 1943

28 | Mrs. Earl Seigle | Martha Spahr | May 10, 1943

29 | Edward D. Rapier | Martha Spahr | May 1943

30 | Mrs. Joseph Susan | Martha Spahr | May 8, 1943

31 | Mrs. F. E. Keith | Martha Spahr | May 9, 1943

32 | Mrs. J. C. Bradford | Martha Spahr | May 10, 1943

33 | Miss Flora L. Hill | Martha Spahr | May 9, 1943

34 | Margaret Fowler | Martha Spahr | May 1943

35 | Herman Winkler | Martha Spahr | May 8, 1943

36 | Walter Duncan | Martha Spahr | May 9, 1943

37 | William E. Coonley | Martha Spahr | May 1943

38 | Mrs. Russ McCann | Martha Spahr | May 9, 1943

39 | Marguerite Costenbader | Martha Spahr | May 10, 1943

40 | Unknown | Martha Spahr | May 1943

41 | Walter Finke | Martha Spahr | May 8, 1943

42 | John Kienitz | Martha Spahr | May 9, 1943

43 | Kathyleen Harper | Martha Spahr | May 10, 1943

44 | Mrs. V. C. Clark | Martha Spahr | May 8, 1943

45 | Mrs. Kenneth Ball | Martha Spahr | May 9, 1943

46 | Arthur Hensen | Martha Spahr | May 9, 1943

47 | Mrs. F. G. Farrell | Martha Spahr | May 8, 1943

48 | Miss Mary Hazelbaker | Martha Spahr | May 10, 1943

49 | Mrs. Alma Hodges | Martha Spahr | May 9, 1943

50 | Magdalene Hoffield | Martha Spahr | May 10, 1943

51 | Hazel P. Woodley | Martha Spahr | May 10, 1943

52 | Mrs. Jean Alvarez | Martha Spahr | May 13, 1943

53 | George Bigler | Martha Spahr | May 9, 1943

54 | Mildred West | Martha Spahr | May 9, 1943

55 | Mrs. F. H. Kahler | Martha Spahr | May 8, 1943

56 | Ted Wholford | Martha Spahr | May 8, 1943

58 | Flavius Jankauskas | Martha Spahr | May 9, 1943 | Published with permission from Flavius Jankauskas

61 | Mrs. Don Yant | Flavius Jankauskas | July 1, 1943 | Published with permission from Flavius Jankauskas

INDEX OF LETTERS

WWII Radio Heroes: Letters of Compassion

Postal Orders

Spahr Consulting, Lisa Spahr, 7731 Abbott Street, Pittsburgh, PA 15221. USA. Send check or credit card details (below) for total due. Include this form.

Web/Email Orders

www.powletters.com
or email
order@powletters.com

Telephone Orders

(412) 867-9991
9 AM – 9 PM
Eastern Standard Time

NUMBER OF COPIES AND SHIPPING COST

		NUMBER OF COPIES			
Please send me *WWII Radio Heroes: Letters of Compassion*		NUMBER OF COPIES	X $ 15.95 per book	=	
Shipping costs	Book rate to continental United States address	NUMBER OF COPIES	X $ 4.00 per book	=	
	International address	NUMBER OF COPIES	X $ 10.00 per book	=	

Total

AUTOGRAPHING AND PERSONALIZING

☐ check this box if you want the book(s) autographed by the author

☐ check this box if you want the book(s) personalized, provide the name to the right (please print legibly to ensure proper duplication)

_____

_____

SHIPPING INFORMATION

Name: _____

Address: _____

City: _____ State: _____ Zip: _____

Telephone: _____ Email: _____

PAYMENT INFORMATION

☐ check this box if paying by check—make check payable to "Spahr Consulting"

☐ check this box if paying by credit card and supply the information below

Card Type: ☐ Visa ☐ MasterCard ☐ Discover

Card Number: _____

Expiration Date: _____ 3-Digit Code on Signature Block _____

Name on Card: _____

LaVergne, TN USA
12 March 2010
175753LV00004B/1/A

9 780976 218173